解析约翰·罗尔斯
《正义论》

AN ANALYSIS OF

JOHN RAWLS'S

A THEORY OF JUSTICE

Filippo Dionigi　Jeremy Kleidosty ◎ 著
高伟　高英淇 ◎ 译

上海外语教育出版社
SHANGHAI FOREIGN LANGUAGE EDUCATION PRESS

目　录

引 言 …………………………………………… 1
　　约翰·罗尔斯其人　　　　　　　　　　　2
　　《正义论》的主要内容　　　　　　　　　3
　　《正义论》的学术价值　　　　　　　　　4

第一部分：学术渊源　　　　　　　　　　　　7
　　1. 作者生平与历史背景　　　　　　　　8
　　2. 学术背景　　　　　　　　　　　　　12
　　3. 主导命题　　　　　　　　　　　　　16
　　4. 作者贡献　　　　　　　　　　　　　20

第二部分：学术思想　　　　　　　　　　　　25
　　5. 思想主脉　　　　　　　　　　　　　26
　　6. 思想支脉　　　　　　　　　　　　　30
　　7. 历史成就　　　　　　　　　　　　　34
　　8. 著作地位　　　　　　　　　　　　　39

第三部分：学术影响　　　　　　　　　　　　43
　　9. 最初反响　　　　　　　　　　　　　44
　　10. 后续争议　　　　　　　　　　　　48
　　11. 当代印迹　　　　　　　　　　　　52
　　12. 未来展望　　　　　　　　　　　　56

术语表 ………………………………………… 59
人名表 ………………………………………… 64

CONTENTS

WAYS IN TO THE TEXT	71
Who Was John Rawls?	72
What Does *A Theory of Justice* Say?	73
Why Does *A Theory of Justice* Matter?	75
SECTION 1: INFLUENCES	79
Module 1: The Author and the Historical Context	80
Module 2: Academic Context	85
Module 3: The Problem	90
Module 4: The Author's Contribution	95
SECTION 2: IDEAS	101
Module 5: Main Ideas	102
Module 6: Secondary Ideas	107
Module 7: Achievement	111
Module 8: Place in the Author's Work	116
SECTION 3: IMPACT	121
Module 9: The First Responses	122
Module 10: The Evolving Debate	127
Module 11: Impact and Influence Today	132
Module 12: Where Next?	137
Glossary of Terms	141
People Mentioned in the Text	148
Works Cited	153

引言

要 点

- 约翰·罗尔斯（1921—2002）是20世纪最具影响力的美国哲学家之一。
- 罗尔斯在第二次世界大战*期间在美军服役。由于这段经历，他广泛撰写有关正义和社会的问题。
- 《正义论》认为社会应追求公平正义*。他鼓励人们想象一个被所有社会阶层视为公平的理论上的社会。

约翰·罗尔斯其人

约翰·罗尔斯，《正义论》（1971）的作者，1921年出生于马里兰州巴尔的摩市一个中上阶层的基督徒家庭。他的父亲是一位著名的律师，他的母亲是当地妇女选民联盟*（该组织有一个基本上进步的政治议程，最初是为了帮助女性在公民生活中发挥更积极的作用而成立的）的主席。

作为普林斯顿大学的本科生，罗尔斯接触到了美国哲学家诺曼·马尔科姆*的观点。马尔科姆曾是奥地利哲学家路德维希·维特根斯坦*的学生，维特根斯坦着迷于语言在人类思维方式中所扮演的角色。这种想法将孕育罗尔斯后来的学术兴趣，即社会定义"正义"一词的含义。

罗尔斯在普林斯顿时期的特点是用浓厚的宗教方法研究政治哲学*。他考虑研究神学并入神职。但是，当罗尔斯20岁时，美国参加第二次世界大战。两年后，罗尔斯在太平洋地区执勤。他在1943年到1946年之间的从军经历使他放弃了他的信仰，寻求另一种方式来构想一个完善的（即正义的）社会。¹他选择政治哲学作为实现这一目标的最佳手段,从此成为一名学者。他在麻省理工学院和康奈尔大学工作,之后于 1962 年在哈佛大学获得职位。

在 2002 年去世前的几十年里,约翰·罗尔斯成为他那一代最有影响力和经常被引用的政治思想家之一。他的第一本书《正义论》于 1971 年出版。这部广受好评的作品引发人们辩论、批评,并受到广泛的推崇,奠定了他作为政治哲学家的声誉。

《正义论》的主要内容

约翰·罗尔斯在《正义论》中的目标是为人们思考正义开辟一条新途径。他想提供一种替代功利主义*哲学的思想。功利主义认为一个行动的善恶应该根据其后果来判断;一个"德性的"行为替最大多数的人带来了最大的善。当罗尔斯撰写《正义论》时,功利主义思想非常受欢迎,但罗尔斯反对这些。他认为功利主义忽视了个人的福祉,只考虑某一行为对大多数人的利益。罗尔斯说,这打开了滥用与痛苦之门。

为了取代功利主义,罗尔斯重振了社会契约*的传统。自由主义*政治传统中的一个关键思想,强调个人自由的重要性,就是社会建立在"国家与该国每个公民之间隐含契约"的观念之上。契约是指个人将放弃他们的一些天然自由(基本上就是他们喜欢随意做任何事情的自由),而作为交换,国家将创建一个保护个人的社会。

罗尔斯的社会图景是由具有正义感的自由和理性的个体组成的群体。这是他著作的潜在假设。他认为,这个社会(被定义为"共同利益的合作事业"[2])的成员将全都同意应该支持公正社会的原则。罗尔斯将正义定义为公平:对他而言,正义应该依赖于每个人都认为公平的条件和程序。³他对正义作为社会"基本结构"的基础感兴趣：核心价值观体现在核心制度中。

罗尔斯认为，一个真正公正的社会是一个所有成员都认为其公正的社会，无论他们的社会阶层或宗教或道德信仰如何。由于很难让任何人从他人的角度想象一个公正的社会会是什么样子，罗尔斯提供工具（思想实验*）来帮助他的读者做出这种同理心的飞跃。⁴他还提供其他想法来帮助每个人反思社会正义及其意义。这些想法包括罗尔斯称为"反思平衡"*的概念——人们通过质疑和重新评估来发展他们对正义的理解，直到达到平衡点为止。⁵

罗尔斯将另一个创新概念称为"差异原则"*。他认为，在一个公正的社会中，如果不平等的财富分配对社会中最弱势的人有利，那么这种不平等就是可以容忍的；激励某个拥有某种能力的人可能是对社会有益的，例如，给某人时间训练成为外科医生，因为他们所做的工作将使社会受益。但罗尔斯对这个论点加了限定，认为赚取不平等财富的手段应该来自基于功德且向任何人开放的工作。⁶

罗尔斯方法的重要性在于其对宗教和文化保持中立的主张：社会的所有成员都应该相信他们的社会是公平的。罗尔斯独特的方法认为人们本身就具有相同的价值，但认识到人们的能力是不平等的。有些人可以为社会做出更多贡献。最后，即使在公正的社会中，也可能存在不平等。

《正义论》的学术价值

罗尔斯的著作以自由政治理论的传统写成，强调普遍人权*的概念，以及每个人的重要性。《正义论》的关键主题是自由主义传统的核心支柱，它们包括正义、个人平等、自由以及理性和公共推理的重要性。他所提出的政治问题是一个反复出现的问题：人们怎样才能在一个最能让所有人过上美好生活的社会中过上最美好的生活？

然而，罗尔斯的一些假设限制了其著作的应用性。《正义论》于1971年出版。在接下来的几十年里，对正义的需求逐渐变为全球的需求，凸显了罗尔斯的理论植根于西方自由主义传统的深度。罗尔斯的正义理论旨在普适。他声称它是普遍吸收和普遍适用的。但它不适合讨论国际关系中的正义。全球贫困、正义战争和宽容是全球政治议程的首要问题，虽然还有关于用什么原则来对一个公正的国际社会加以规范以及应该对其他国家的人民承担什么样的道德义务的辩论，但这些问题只在罗尔斯正义理论中得到简要概述。他的著作主要涉及法律制度等国内民主社会制度，但这些制度在国际关系中较不发达。此外，也缺乏如何在这些背景下分享权力的统一认识。

尽管罗尔斯的方法受到限制，但《正义论》创造了许多新思想，这些思想仍然有助于思考政治。在发表了40多年后，罗尔斯的著作在一系列问题的讨论中反复被提到：从人权、民主化*和宽容*，到发展*、多元主义*和宪政主义*与民主化。

罗尔斯的理论在发表时引发了广泛的争论。辩论仍在进行中。但即使是那些反对他的观点的人也为他的作品喝彩；例如，罗尔斯思想的批评者、美国哲学家迈克尔·桑德尔*说：《正义论》是"值得庆祝的。"[7]

1. 埃里克·格雷戈里:"在原初状态之前:年轻的约翰·罗尔斯的新东正教神学",《宗教伦理学杂志》第35卷,2007年第2期,第195—196页。
2. 约翰·罗尔斯:《正义论》,坎布里奇:哈佛大学贝尔纳普出版社,1999年,第4页。
3. 罗尔斯在其理论之前的第一批重要出版物是他的文章"作为公平的正义",《哲学评论》第67卷,1958年第2期。
4. 见罗尔斯:《正义论》,第118—122页。
5. 罗尔斯:《正义论》,第17—19页。
6. 罗尔斯:《正义论》,第72页。
7. 迈克尔·桑德尔:《自由主义和正义的限制》(第2版),剑桥:剑桥大学出版社,1998年,第9页。

第一部分：学术渊源

1 作者生平与历史背景

要点

- 约翰·罗尔斯的开创性著作《正义论》是过去50年来最具影响力的政治哲学著作之一。
- 在罗尔斯的童年时代,他的两个兄弟死亡,他的母亲致力于妇女权利的工作,他与贫穷或少数民族家庭的孩子交友,这些都影响了他。
- 罗尔斯在第二次世界大战中的经历促使他对正义概念产生了兴趣。

为何要读这部著作?

约翰·罗尔斯的著作《正义论》于1971年首次出版。它创立了一个新的政治哲学学派——罗尔斯主义,并产生了一系列有关正义以及"正义"含义的学术思想。罗尔斯的思想和方法引起了持续的讨论。

罗尔斯的著作被认为如此重要的一个原因是它提供了功利主义哲学的替代品。功利主义从整个社会的角度看待正义:它的支持者认为,应该通过考虑哪种结果将为最多的人提供最大的善来做出决定。这种方法在集体社会利益的背景下考虑正义,但忽视了个人的需要。相比之下,罗尔斯从个人的角度探讨了正义。对于罗尔斯来说,正义要求每个人都被"公平地"对待:享受基本的生活标准,并被给予在社会中升迁的机会。

1971年之后很难找到一部与他的作品无关的政治理论著作。《正义论》已经出版了两个版本,有20多种语言版本。罗尔斯认为，他的想法可以在任何时间和任何地方普遍适用。译本的数量支持这一论点，因为来自许多不同国家、政治制度和宗教传统的学者不断地阅读和提及他的著作。

> "我经常思考为什么我的宗教信仰发生了变化，特别是在战争期间。我本来是一个信奉正统圣公会教的基督徒，而在1945年6月时完全放弃信仰。……有三件事凸显在我的记忆中：克雷山脊*事件、迪肯的死以及对大屠杀*的了解和反思。"[1]
>
> ——约翰·罗尔斯：《我的宗教观》

作者生平

1921年，罗尔斯出生于美国马里兰州巴尔的摩市，他来自一个中上阶层家庭。他的父母都是基督徒，并积极参与政治。他的父亲是民主党的一员，参与当地政府和政治活动，他的母亲积极参与当地的妇女权利运动。但悲剧袭击了这个家庭。小时候，罗尔斯失去了两个患白喉和肺炎疾病的弟弟，他们是从他那里感染的。可悲的是，这些死亡事件相继发生在一年之内，给罗尔斯留下了持久的印象——生命既短暂又天生地不公平。[2]

罗尔斯进了教会学校，在那里他取得了优异的成绩，年轻的他考虑加入神职人员并进行神学研究，但他最终决定学习哲学和公共道德。在获得普林斯顿大学的本科学位后，他于1943年加入美军，并在第二次世界大战中参战，尔后返回普林斯顿大学完成博士学位。后来获得富布赖特奖学金去牛津大学访学，在那里他遇到了几位创新思想家：有影响力的法律哲学家哈特*、自由主义*哲学家以赛亚·伯林*和政治哲学家斯图尔特·汉普希尔*。[3] 这些学者在20世纪50年代关于政治理论的辩论中起着核心作用,对罗尔斯有着关键影响。[4]

他的思想也受到当时世界事件的影响。第二次世界大战接近尾声时,罗尔斯被派驻日本。广岛*被核武器轰炸(战争中首次使用核武器)、纳粹大屠杀(在此过程中,纳粹*杀害了大约1 100万欧洲人,其中大部分是犹太人)和后来爆发的越南战争*(罗尔斯积极反对)深刻地影响了他。[5]

创作背景

1971年,当《正义论》首次出版时,美国社会正在经历快速变化,其中出现了不同社会群体之间的暴力冲突。就在几年前,美国目睹了民权运动*的兴起,这一社会运动成功地将美国少数种族群体的苦难带到了民族意识的最前沿。在国际上,美国全神贯注于越南战争。美国代表南越对抗北越的冲突第一次在电视上播出,美国公众第一次接触到暴力的战争现实。到20世纪60年代后期,冲突已经分裂了社会,许多人质疑美国的正义思想,社会公平感被彻底动摇——这在《正义论》中显而易见。

但人们还意识到在协同努力实现共同目标时可以取得的成就。20世纪60年代,是经历巨大动荡的十年,也是一个取得伟大社会成就和理想主义的时代。1965年,林登·约翰逊*总统签署了民权法案*,使其成为法律。所有公民第一次被承诺获得平等机会:人们可以投票、做生意和上学而不受种族歧视。四年后,1969年7月,阿波罗号登月。美国人正在实现十年前被认为不可能的事情。

《正义论》生逢其时。罗尔斯质疑关于善和正义的基本假设,同时相信,它们有可能通过合作而实现。

1. 迪肯是罗尔斯的朋友，他也参加了第二次世界大战。
2. 托马斯·温弗里德·波格和米歇尔·科施：《约翰·罗尔斯生平与正义论》，伦敦：牛津大学出版社，2007年，第5页。
3. 波格和科施：《约翰·罗尔斯》，第16页。
4. 例如，罗尔斯在提出对正义概念和可能在不同人之间重现的各种正义概念之间的区别时提到了哈特；约翰·罗尔斯：《正义论（修订版）》，坎布里奇：哈佛大学贝尔纳普出版社，1999年，第5页。更通俗地说，罗尔斯使用哈特理论来定义其理论的几个关键概念。同样，柏林被用作自由概念及其定义辩论的参考；罗尔斯：《正义论》，第177页。
5. 后来，他将发表一篇文章，反对在广岛和东京对平民使用滥杀滥伤武器。见约翰·罗尔斯，"广岛之后50年"，《异议》，1995年夏，第323—327页。

2 学术背景

要点

- 政治理论关注构成任何社会基础的思想。政治理论家通常试图想象如何创造一个帮助人们过上"美好生活"的社会。
- 主要的政治理论学派包括功利主义(为最多的人寻求最大的善)、自由主义(为个人寻求最大的善)以及契约主义(通过个人与国家签订合同以换取国家提供"美好生活"的手段)。
- 罗尔斯遵循了自由主义和契约主义的传统。

著作语境

当约翰·罗尔斯于1971年出版《正义论》时,政治理论的学术领域面临着严峻的挑战。国际关系随后被定义为冷战*——美国和苏联之间的长期紧张局势。国与国结盟,分为资本主义*世界与共产主义世界;全世界各国都被迫在这场意识形态战争中选择一个阵营。两个阵营都认为他们知道建立社会秩序的正确方法。他们都以功利主义哲学为基础来论证他们的观点,认为虽然有些人会不可避免地难以受益,但是他们的制度将为大多数人取得尽可能最好的结果。

但罗尔斯想要一种能够在不伤害个人的情况下创造良好社会结果的政治理论。他清楚地说:"正如每个人都必须通过理性反省决定什么构成他的善……一群人必须一劳永逸地决定在他们中间什么是正义的和不正义的。"[1]

为了找到一条处于现有极端政治思想之间的路径,罗尔斯转向了社会契约，该思想可以在英国哲学家约翰·洛克*和瑞士出生的哲学家让－雅克·卢梭*等思想家的著作中找到。社会契约是个人之间合作的隐含协议，以创造一个互利的社会。但是，在德国哲学家伊曼纽尔·康德*的传统中，罗尔斯增加了道德和伦理方面的维度。他的出发点是个人在社会中拥有公正和公平生活的理性愿望。[2]在《正义论》中，他设计了一个体系，让社会可以用来确定什么是正义。罗尔斯认为这个体系可以在任何时候适用于任何社会。

> "我的目的是提出一种正义观，这种正义观进一步概括人们所熟悉的社会契约理论，比方说洛克、卢梭和康德提出的契约论，并使之上升到一个更高的抽象水平。"
> ——约翰·罗尔斯：《正义论》

学科概览

罗尔斯经常提到康德。康德是一位极具影响力的思想家，因其伦理著作而闻名，如《道德形而上学》（1797）。在书中，康德使用假设情境来表明（理性的）人们如何构建可以在整个社会中被接受的道德观念。罗尔斯倾向于同意康德的看法，即理性的人是"自主的道德代理人"——也就是说，个人可以自由地用自己的方式思考善与恶。罗尔斯还使用了康德的一个关键方法：将读者置于虚拟的情境中，并从理论的角度要求他们描述怎样才算一个公正、公平和善良的国家。[3]

罗尔斯明确表示，《正义论》试图提供一种替代功利主义的政治理论观点。在他的著作导言中，他认为功利主义在很大程度上是因为最先提出来这一思想的人的才华而变得流行。罗尔斯说，英国哲学家大卫·休谟*、亚当·史密斯*和杰里米·边沁*都是"一流的社会理论家和经济学家"。但他也认为，他们的道德理论缺乏明确性。在很多情况下，很难将道德与严格的社会效用相协调。

例如，按照边沁的思想，一个缺乏食物或资金的国家可能会决定让社会中最弱或生产力最低的成员死去，这将有助于国家为那些能够积极为社会做出贡献的人提供资源。但罗尔斯说，大多数人会反对牺牲老人和病人的想法。大多数社会会给予这些群体特别的关注和考虑。罗尔斯在《正义论》中所表述的目的是创造一种"可行和系统的道德观来抗衡（功利主义）。"[4]

学术渊源

约翰·罗尔斯对影响他著作的人和哲学持开放态度。他的目标是提供正义的定义，并借此帮助人们创造公正的社会。历史上的思想家都以此为目标。事实上，罗尔斯写道："主导思想是经典的和众所周知的。"洛克在17世纪就讨论了个人与国家之间存在契约的概念。他认为，人们订立这份契约，是因为他们相信国家将为他们提供保障"生命，自由和财产"的能力。[5] 洛克的思想得到了卢梭思想的补充，卢梭认为人是天生自由的，但被社会奴役。卢梭认为，社会不允许个人管理自己或拥有自己的道德价值观。

康德提供了这个思想链中的最后一环。他认为人不应该被视为达到目的的手段，而应作为目的本身——他称之为绝对命令*。对于康德来说，这种方法提供了一个基础，人们可以从中理性地思考他们希望如何被他人对待，他对如何保护每个人的尊严感兴趣。

这些哲学家对罗尔斯的思想产生了深远的影响，但罗尔斯也是牛津大学和哈佛大学充满活力的知识分子之一。他提到了影响他思想的一些同代人。这些人包括著名学者：印度出生的哲学家阿马蒂亚·森*、美国哲学家罗伯特·诺齐克*和拉脱维亚出生的政治理论家朱迪思·什克拉*。[6] 虽然诺齐克批评了罗尔斯的观点，但罗尔斯承认他发现这些批评很有用。相比之下，森和什克拉都在自己的著作中使用了罗尔斯的一些观点。[7]

---

1. 约翰·罗尔斯：《正义论（修订版）》，坎布里奇：哈佛大学贝尔纳普出版社，1999 年，第 10—11 页。
2. 罗尔斯：《正义论》，第 10—12 页。同时见他早期的著作《作为公平的正义》，《哲学评论》第 67 卷，1958 年第 2 期，第 164—191 页。
3. 罗尔斯：《正义论》，第 10—11 页。
4. 罗尔斯：《正义论》，序言第 18 页。
5. 约翰·洛克：《论政府的两篇论文》，彼得·拉斯莱特译，剑桥：剑桥大学出版社，1988 年，第 323 页。
6. 罗尔斯：《正义论》，序言第 21 页。
7. 参见阿马蒂亚·森：《论经济不平等》，牛津：牛津大学出版社，1973 年；罗伯特·诺齐克："分配正义"，《哲学与公共事务》，1973 年，第 45—126 页；朱迪思·什克拉："公平评述非正义"，《耶鲁法律杂志》，1989 年，第 1135—1151 页。

3 主导命题

要点

- 约翰·罗尔斯在《正义论》中试图定义"正义"并为社会提供有助于使其变得更加公正的工具。
- 在撰写《正义论》时,最流行的正义观是功利主义:正义即被认为是为最多数人实现良好结果的命题。
- 为了创造一种可以在任何时间或地点适用于任何一群人的正义理论,罗尔斯驳斥了功利主义,因为它不保护个人的权利。

核心问题

约翰·罗尔斯在《正义论》中提出的中心问题是:公正社会应该建立什么样的原则?在书中,罗尔斯证明了这个问题的重要性。任何社会都基于共同的思想。这些想法的基础应该是什么? 罗尔斯的回答是:真理。如何在社会制度中保护和体现真理? 他的答案是:通过正义。通过将哲学中的真理与社会制度中的正义作类比,罗尔斯说明了他所探究的核心问题。正义(维护真理)是社会的基本美德。因此,致力于使社会变得更好的思想家理所当然将其作为探究对象。[1]

当罗尔斯写作时,功利主义思想在政治哲学领域占主导地位。功利主义认为,当一个制度为整个社会实现了理想的利益时,正义就实现了。虽然这个论点忽视了个人,但是确实,完全个人主义的理论不会促进平等或公平。

罗尔斯采用一种新颖的社会契约理论的方法来解决这个问题。

他说,一个国家的每个人都是平等的公民。每个人都可以思考一个国家怎样才能提供平等机会和公平。他说所有公民都应享有平等的自由(法律规定下的平等自由)和机会平等。这意味着:虽然有些人会比其他人获得更多,但是这将以公平(即公正)的方式发生。

> "现在应尽可能从平等公民地位的角度评估基本结构。这一地位的标志是平等自由原则和公平机会平等原则所要求的权利和自由。当这两个原则得到满足时,所有人都是平等的公民,所以每个人都拥有这一地位。"
> ——约翰·罗尔斯:《正义论》

参与者

当罗尔斯撰写《正义论》时,大多数政治理论家都在使用功利主义的方法(这种方法的基础假设是,任何特定的政治制度应该根据其为尽可能多的人创造良好结果的能力来判断)研究正义。例如,英国哲学家乔纳森·哈里森*写道,实现正义的普遍责任需要一种普遍适用的理论,这种理论只能在功利主义中找到。其他几位作家,其中包括英国经济学家哈罗德*,试图修改古典功利主义,增加现代社会科学、经济学和更加细致入微的道德体系。同样,英国哲学家亨利·西季威克*试图证明功利主义是一种道德理论,可以应用于探讨经济和社会正义问题。[2]

虽然这些思想家中的大多数都意识到功利主义可以用来以共同利益的名义为暴行找借口,但他们认为这是创造社会有益政治制度的最佳方式。他们试图找到处理功利主义所造成的道德困境的方法,而不是试图产生另一种政治理论。对道德的关注一直是功利主义思想家的核心。英国哲学家大卫·休谟和杰里米·边沁是这一思想流派的主要支持者，他们在作品的标题中明确提到了道德。休谟撰写了《道德原理探究》(1751)，而边沁撰写了《道德与立法原理》(1789)。[3]

当代论战

在《正义论》中，罗尔斯主张反对功利主义思想和他所谓的"直觉主义"*。他认为，基于功利主义的社会依赖于人类的直觉来知道它何时将跨越一个不应该跨越的道德或伦理界限。罗尔斯说这种观点"虽然不无道理，且我们也没有把握一定能得出另一种更好的观点，但是没有理由不试一试"。[4]

罗尔斯指出，直觉主义意味着人们依靠他们的原则来确定边界是否即将被侵犯。但直觉主义并没有提供任何方法或规则来决定哪些原则是最重要的。这意味着人们很容易持有相互冲突的原则，从而无法创造出理性的（或普遍的）道德。罗尔斯特别提到了美国哲学家罗伯特·诺齐克的批评。在他的《道德困境和道德结构》中，诺齐克指出，对于什么是"不言而喻"，什么是"必要的道德原则"，人们可以得出截然不同的结论。[5]

但罗尔斯并不是简单地批判功利主义或直觉主义思想。在《正义论》中，他提供了另一种思维方式。为了确定特定系统的公正性，他提出了两个关键原则：

- 定义基本自由的规则应"平等地适用于每个人"。人们应该在不干扰别人自由的前提下拥有最大的自由。
- 在制度允许不平等的情况下，只有为了使每个人受益，才该这么做。[6]例如，如果有人受到激励，去做对社会有用的和惠及他人的工作，所有人可能会同意：如果不平等存在，他们会更好。

虽然罗尔斯的思想基于传统的社会契约理论（即自由主义思想：如果国家能够保障安全和政治权利，放弃某些自由是值得的），但也为政治理论提供了一种新的和另辟蹊径的方法。

---

1. 约翰·罗尔斯：《正义论（修订版）》，坎布里奇：哈佛大学贝尔纳普出版社，1999年，第3页。
2. 参见罗尔斯：《正义论》，第20页脚注。
3. 罗尔斯：《正义论》，第20页脚注。
4. 罗尔斯：《正义论》，序言第18页。
5. 罗尔斯：《正义论》，第30页。
6. 罗尔斯：《正义论》，第56页。

4 作者贡献

要点

- 罗尔斯在《正义论》中的主要目标是为人们创造一种新的理性方式来建立一个公正公平的社会。
- 罗尔斯展示了他如何得出他的结论，让读者理解他是如何形成他的正义观的。
- 罗尔斯并不要求人们接受他对正义的定义，他只是提供了一个系统来帮助社会定义他们对正义的理解。

作者目标

约翰·罗尔斯的著作《正义论》是用自由主义的政治理论写成的。罗尔斯提出了一种正义理论，认为个人是道德理性的代理（能够根据理性思维在道德上行事），并支持绝对自由的原则。他的著作集中体现了人权的普遍概念。对于罗尔斯而言，这些权利优先于在多元社会（即允许差异的社会，特别是在政治信仰方面）中可以找到的不同道德立场。

这些自由主义、多元主义的价值观是罗尔斯两个关键原则的基础：

- 平等自由原则。根据该原则，"每个人对与其他人所拥有的最广泛的平等基本自由体系相容的类似自由体系都应有一种平等的权利"。[1]换言之，只要个人的自由不会损害他人的自由，他们就应该有行动自由。
- 差异原则。一个公正社会中的商品分配不均，只要有利于该社会中最弱势的人，就可以容忍。此外，这些不平等必须来自对所有人开放的职位和职务。

罗尔斯承认他继承了德国哲学家伊曼纽尔·康德所体现的自由主义思想传统。[2] 他的理论与康德和瑞士出生的哲学家让-雅克·卢梭的社会契约思想部分相同。[3] 然而，罗尔斯的思想也具有开创性。与康德不同，罗尔斯声称他的正义原则不是抽象的，而是扎根于分析并可以复制。罗尔斯也以一种新的方式研究社会契约的概念。他用它作为工具来帮助人们思考特定社会结构的合法性。本质上，罗尔斯声称他的哲学方法更接近科学而非艺术。

> "我试图将正义理论作为一种可行的系统学说提出来，这样，最大化善的观念不会因理论缺失而处于支配地位。对目的论*理论的批评不能单独有成效地进行。我们必须尝试构建另一种观点，它具有相同的清晰度和系统性的优点，但会对我们的道德感受产生更具鉴别力的解释。"
>
> ——约翰·罗尔斯：《正义论》

研究方法

罗尔斯解释了他的目标。他讨论了构想一个公平社会的其他方法，并解释了他对这些方法的反对意见。然后，他仔细而有条不紊地定义了许多概念和工具——"思想实验"——帮助读者理解他的推理并测试他的想法。罗尔斯的假设是：他的正义观可以普遍适用；任何时候、任何社会都可以承认其为理性的。

罗尔斯创造的概念包括："原初状态"*[4]、"无知之幕"*和"反思均衡"*。

根据"原初状态"，如果理性的人有块空白的画布来创造一个新的社会，他们会希望社会实现什么？他们怎样才能最好地创造出一个符合这些目标的社会？

凭借"无知之幕"，罗尔斯让我们有机会考虑一个公平的社会对其最弱势的成员意味着什么。他促使他的读者思考如何在毫不了解自己的社会地位的状态下建立一个社会。无知之幕假定"没有人知道他在社会中的地位——他的阶级地位或社会地位，也没有人知道他在先天资质和能力、智力、体能等方面的命运"。[5]

最后，"反思均衡"要求读者通过来回检查他们的想法直到达到平衡点来重新评估他们先前持有的原则。[6]

这些哲学训练有助于人们定义"正义"。罗尔斯质疑历史具有"特定目的"的观点：这种假设存在于许多哲学中。他还挑战自由主义和社会契约理论的正统观念，即有关人性的基本真理使正义受到限制。罗尔斯认为，正义可以通过人类的反思来创造。

时代贡献

罗尔斯并不是第一个讨论正义概念的政治理论家。他也不是第一个根据"社会中什么对个人有益"来定义"正义"的人。他发展了像约翰·洛克这样有影响力的英国政治哲学家的著作思想，洛克认为政府可以通过被统治者的同意来统治。洛克认为，个人这样做是为了获得自然权利的安全：生命、自由和财产。社会契约传统意味着一个不保护这些自然权利的政府是非法的。但罗尔斯更进了一步。他声称人们天然是平等的；我们可以通过想象自己在原初状态下的无知之幕的背后，来证明所有人都应该被视为平等公民。

罗尔斯的方法将社会契约传统与康德之后的观念相结合，即个人是人们应该在这些问题中考虑的主要单位。在神学传统中，人的自我中心是一个弱点。对于罗尔斯来说，它是人类的一个方面，可以用来让人们不那么自私地思考。通过想象自己可能处于特定社会的底层，人们就会努力创造一个对所有成员都公平的社会。

在个人与社会、实践与道德的结合中，罗尔斯是一位非常独特的思想家。他从洛克和康德获得灵感，并以杰里米·边沁和大卫·休谟的思想作对比，创造了他自己的理性思考正义的创新体系。

---

1. 约翰·罗尔斯：《正义论（修订版）》，坎布里奇：哈佛大学贝尔纳普出版社，1999 年，第 53 页。
2. 罗尔斯：《正义论》，第 221—227 页。
3. 罗尔斯：《正义论》，第 10 页。
4. 罗尔斯：《正义论》，第 118—122 页。
5. 罗尔斯：《正义论》，第 10—11 页。
6. 罗尔斯：《正义论》，第 17—19 页。

第二部分：学术思想

5 思想主脉

要点

- 罗尔斯研究了正义理论、公正社会和政府的制度以及一个公正社会的理想结果。
- 罗尔斯的主要论点是：人们可以通过为最不富裕的人定义一个可接受的公平社会来合理地推导出正义原则。
- 罗尔斯的目的是在正义问题上运用哲学和科学的方法；他的目标是使他的著作理性和普遍适用。

核心主题

在《正义论》中，约翰·罗尔斯将"正义"定义为"公平"。他认为公正社会本质上是一个公民身份平等、机会平等的公平社会。为了探索这些观点，他采用了一种他称之为"反思均衡"的方法。[1] 他概述一个特定的政治问题或辩论，审查有关该主题的意见，分析它们的优点和缺点，然后根据这些优点和缺点调整自己的想法。这个过程使他自己的理论更加平衡和坚实。他将自己的著作分为三个部分：正义理论、公正社会和政府的制度以及公正社会的目标（期望的结果）。

罗尔斯对功利主义政治理论的不满促使他撰写了《正义论》。他认为，尽管功利主义主张道德，但这一哲学可能导致非常不道德的政策，因为它不能为人们提供优先考虑不同美德的方法，或是决定他们社会可以追求的美德的方法。他还指出，关于什么对社会最有益，功利主义没有提供任何机制来达成共识。

直觉主义的主观性（大致是通过使用直觉来衡量每一方的论证来解决某些哲学问题的过程）意味着它不能被合理地用于将道德推理转化为社会政策。罗尔斯概述了功利主义的弱点，并提供了他自己的观点：自由必须尽可能宽泛，只有当一个人的行动自由干扰到别人的自由时才受限。

> "第一：每个人对与其他人所拥有的最广泛的平等基本自由体系相容的类似自由体系都应有一种平等的权利。第二：社会和经济不平等应这样安排，使它们（1）被合理地期望符合每一个人的利益；并且（2）依系于向所有人开放的职位和职务。"
> ——约翰·罗尔斯：《正义论》

思想探究

罗尔斯的著作在开篇概述了从欧洲思想史上的启蒙运动*（大约在17世纪中叶到19世纪初）到工业时代*（开始于18世纪中期，从以农业为基础的社会转变为以工业为基础的社会）期间功利主义和直觉主义思想的演变。

他认为，要创造一个公平的社会，人们需要想象*如果他们不知道自己在社会中的角色是什么*，他们会创造什么样的社会。他把这称为"原初状态"。这需要一种他所谓的"无知之幕"的假想无知。这是一个要求苛刻的过程：很难想象一个人可能处于社会的绝对底层。这就好像罗尔斯要求他的读者戴上眼罩，滤清思想，然后在一个完全想象的社会中定位自己。[2]

罗尔斯认为，通过这样做，公正社会的两个关键原则变得不言而喻：所有人在法律面前必须是平等的公民，社会差异和不平等只有在为整个社会创造更理想的结果时才能被接受；要被接受的话，必须确保任何人都有可能得到更高的地位或更高薪的工作。[3] 这通常被称为"差异原则"。

罗尔斯将他的方法的假设和结果与功利主义的假设和结果进行了比较。

虽然罗尔斯著作的第一部分本质上是哲学的，但第二部分显然是政治性的。在这里，罗尔斯定义了自由并讨论了它的局限性，他的观点与哲学家约翰·洛克的观点非常相似。[4] 然而，罗尔斯创新的方法是将这些思想与伊曼纽尔·康德之后的伦理学思想结合起来。这些使他的著作具有道德上的弦外之音：对于罗尔斯来说，将正义与公平、个人自由等同起来不仅是合理的事情，而且是*正确的*事情。本部分的内容着眼于经济学、商品分配和社会责任等问题。罗尔斯论及的问题包括公民不服从（一种有意违反某些法律的抗议形式）和依良心拒绝（决定因良心不在军队中服务），反映了美国民权运动和越南战争等事件的影响。

在第三部分中，罗尔斯提供了一种基于理性、不可知论和演绎而不是宗教思想来思考道德的方法。然而，批评者认为他的道德推理不是客观的，而只是反映了罗尔斯自己的主观道德偏好。罗尔斯本人讨论了心理学*的观点和人类寻找意义的愿望。[5]

语言表述

《正义论》的文本非常深奥。罗尔斯的受众是同行哲学家和学者。他认为他的读者熟悉关键的政治理论，并且已经了解这些传统中最重要的思想家。他经常穿梭于哲学、类比和对历史哲学的讨论之间，同时引入复杂的方法来定义复杂的概念。这部著作是多年来集大成之作，并且参考了读者对他早期著作提出的批评。

罗尔斯最重要的论点，他对"公平正义"的定义可以追溯到1958年。这是他第一次引入这一术语的那一年，用它作为《哲学评论》中一篇文章的标题。他的大部分工作起源于为学术期刊撰写的论文，本书反映了这一点。此书使用专业术语，结构复杂，经常使用脚注提供文本证据或进一步解释。这种缜密的方法使他的思想在学术界得到了关注和信誉。罗尔斯的书如此严谨，即使那些从根本上不同意它的人也不得不解释他们为何不同意此书观点。

从这个意义上，可以说这本书具有很大的影响力。事实上，《正义论》的成功让罗尔斯成为为数不多的政治理论家之一，他的想法（不时）被政治家和政府官员认可。

---

1. 约翰·罗尔斯：《正义论（修订版）》，坎布里奇：哈佛大学贝尔纳普出版社，1999年，第17—19页。
2. 罗尔斯：《正义论》，第15—18页。
3. 罗尔斯：《正义论》，第52—64页。
4. 参见理查德·弗农主编：《约翰·洛克论宽容》，剑桥：剑桥大学出版社，2010年，以了解罗尔斯对"社会中应有多少宽容和自由"的看法。
5. 罗尔斯：《正义论》，第429—433页。

6 思想支脉

> 要点
>
> - 罗尔斯著作中次要观点的关键是"原初状态"的概念：可以创造公正社会的空白画布。
> - 一些学者研究过罗尔斯的工具和概念，认为它们本身就是有价值的。
> - 虽然《正义论》的第三部分被低估了，但是人们对罗尔斯著作这部分的学术兴趣日益增加。

其他思想

约翰·罗尔斯的《正义论》中最重要的次要观点之一是被他称为"原初状态"的思想实验——一种富有想象力的训练，他用其得出关于正义性质及其与国家关系的结论。罗尔斯使用了一些技巧来帮助他的读者超越他或她对自己社会地位的认识，让他们考虑真正的正义是什么样的，无论他们在社会中占据什么位置。他称这种缺乏对地位（财富状况、职业、能力、智力，乃至个人道德偏好）的认识为"无知之幕"，认为采用原初状态的思想家可以就正义的本质达成共识。这是因为原初状态"排除了对那些会使人们陷入争论并让他们受到偏见指引的偶发性事件的认知。"[1]

书中的另一个关键思想是"反思均衡"的概念：回归观点，反思其优点和缺点，并在这些优缺点的基础上对观点进行调整。虽然这个概念在文中没有详细讨论，但它的影响遍及罗尔斯所做的每一个论点。虽然《正义论》是一本很长且在某种程度上内容重复的著作，但重复发生的原因是罗尔斯提炼他的思想以达到反思均衡点（用了大约500页的论述来实现）。

很难孤立地谈论罗尔斯的次要思想。它们紧密交织在一起，罗尔斯将它们作为工具向读者展示他的思想是如何发展的。换言之，他的次要思想理清了他的公平正义思想的内容。

> "我们可以将自尊（或自重）定义为有两个方面。首先，正如我们前面提到的，它包括一个人认识到自己的价值，并坚信自己对善有正确认知，自己的生活计划值得执行。其次，自尊意味着一个人有信心在自己能力范围内，运用其才能达到目标。"
>
> ——约翰·罗尔斯:《正义论》

思想探究

罗尔斯认为，他的原初状态的概念对于帮助人们得出关于社会正义的理性的、普适的结论至关重要。他强调原初状态是一个假设的构念。然而，这个想法一直被批评为无法想象。罗尔斯回答说，"原初状态的假设性质引发了一个问题：为什么我们应该对它有任何兴趣，道德或非道德的？回想一下答案：这种情况描述所体现的条件是我们事实上接受的。或者如果我们不接受，那么我们可以通过间或提出的哲学思考来说服我们去接受。"[2]

从这句话可以看出罗尔斯非常有信心。罗尔斯多年来一直在思考正义。他的方法是谨慎和有条不紊的。因此，他（在很大程度上）认为其他人如果同样谨慎地反思这些问题将得出相同的结论。

那么，为什么还要用原初状态的思想实验呢？因为我们已经接受了它的前提，即使我们不这样做，罗尔斯也可以说服我们它们是正确的。

从这个意义上说，罗尔斯的理论冒着成为意识形态本体的危险：一种对世界的看法，这种看法对其假设极其肯定，并提出了强势的训令。

被忽视之处

《正义论》的第三部分是罗尔斯文本中最被忽视的部分之一。[3] 罗尔斯讨论了与道德心理学相关的正义，并引入了"正义情感"的观念——构成特定社会的个人有着共同的正义观。在此讨论之后，罗尔斯着眼于探讨一个对正义有共同理解的社会会成为什么样。他认为，当一个社会关于正义的观念与他们的社会价值观相一致时，该社会可以被称为秩序良好。一个秩序良好的社会可能会享有稳定。罗尔斯还声称，当人们有共同的正义情感时，它有助于社会继续致力于将正义视为共同利益。

直到最近，学者才对罗尔斯的这一部分理论表现出兴趣。一个相关的例子是美国哲学家保罗·魏斯曼*的著作。[4] 他的著作论述了罗尔斯如何从他最初的正义理论转向他后来讨论政治自由主义的著作。[5] 魏斯曼认为，《正义论》不像许多其他学者所认为的那般带有个人主义和康德主义——建立在伊曼纽尔·康德的思想基础上——的色彩。他使用罗尔斯关于稳定和正义情感的观点来表明罗尔斯的哲学依赖于"正义感"。[6] 这指的是人们发展共同道德的能力，良好秩序社会的稳定性就是基于这种道德。

1. 约翰·罗尔斯:《正义论(修订版)》,坎布里奇:哈佛大学贝尔纳普出版社,1999年,第15—17页。
2. 罗尔斯:《正义论》,第514页。
3. 罗尔斯:《正义论》,第347—514页。
4. 保罗·J.威斯曼,《为何选择政治自由主义? 关于约翰·罗尔斯的政治转向》,纽约和牛津:牛津大学出版社,2011年。
5. 特别是在约翰·罗尔斯的论文集中,《政治自由主义》,纽约:哥伦比亚大学出版社,1993年。
6. 根据罗尔斯的观点,"正义感是运用正义原则即按照正义观点去行动的有效欲望",罗尔斯:《正义论》,第497页。

7 历史成就

要点

- 罗尔斯想让别人相信他的正义方法是合理、理性和可实现的（至少在理论上是这样）。
- 需要认真关注其思想的精辟解释、其思考理想社会的工具及其哲学论证的质量。
- 虽然罗尔斯影响了关于正义的辩论，并成为这一领域最重要的思想家之一，但他受到了对自由主义传统及其普遍主义假设（即其假设认为其论据适用于所有情况）依赖的局限。

观点评价

在《正义论》中，约翰·罗尔斯认为他的理论适用于秩序井然的社会——但可能并非世界上所有的社会都反映了罗尔斯"有序的标准。"[1]

一个例子就是一个层级社会，其特点是一个总体道德概念，影响其结构（例如，一个君主制，其中存在社会不平等，而这种不平等不是由其公民的优点和能力产生的）。然而，这个社会仍然可以保证其成员享有相当程度的基本权利。[2] 罗尔斯在他后来的著作《万民法》中讨论了这种可能性。他用一个想象的例子：卡赞尼斯坦国。罗尔斯认为，自由主义者不应该干涉这个社会的事务，因为这会违反自由主义的宽容原则。这个例子显示出罗尔斯理论具有普遍有效性观点的局限性。

美国政治理论家查尔斯·贝茨*和德国哲学家涛慕思·博格*

等学者（以不同的方式）论证了罗尔斯关于平等自由和差异原则的理论可以普遍适用；与罗尔斯本人不同，贝茨和博格认为国家之间的文化差异并不一定代表对承认普遍人权可能性的限制，例如社会和经济权利以及全球社会正义。在《万民法》中，罗尔斯认为只有基本人权才具有普遍性。

> "在不否认理想的实际政治成就很重要的情况下，他（罗尔斯）认为，对其可实现性的充分信赖可以使我们与世界和解。只要我们有理由相信人类的自我维持和公正的集体生活是现实可能的，我们可能希望我们或其他人有朝一日，能在某个地方实现它——然后也可以努力实现这一成就……政治哲学可以提供一种灵感，可以消除无可奈何和愤世嫉俗的危险，甚至可以提升我们今天的生活价值。"
>
> ——涛慕思·博格：《约翰·罗尔斯：生平与正义论》

当时的成就

即使那些不同意罗尔斯的人也赞美他的作品。加拿大出生的马克思主义哲学家杰拉尔德·科恩*是他最尖刻的评论家之一，他写道，"西方政治哲学史上最多有两本书被认为比《正义论》更重要：柏拉图*的《理想国》和霍布斯*的《利维坦》。"3《正义论》一出版就被认为是一部重要的文献。罗尔斯的思想将政治理论的焦点从"共同利益"的功利主义概念转向了个人的利益。

罗尔斯的写作正处在冷战期间——长期的军事和外交紧张局势，在一定程度上，以民主意识形态（美国及其盟国的"西方集团"）和共产主义（苏联*及其盟国的"东方集团"）相互竞争为特征。他试图让政治理论摆脱对功利主义道德哲学和直觉主义*方法

（根据这种方法，直觉是通过权衡替代解决方案来解决哲学问题过程中的有用工具）的依赖。

相反，他的目的是创造一种自由主义和契约主义*的关于正义的理解：一种基于自由的理解，以及我们通过合同同意某些义务来商定社会生活状况的观点，这种观点可以得到普遍认同和实现。[4]

虽然他如愿摆脱了功利主义对政治理论的束缚，但他的思想为创造正义提供普遍蓝图这一愿望，还未被全球政治的后续发展所彻底检验。普遍性并不总是政治理论的目标，也不是每个社会都希望实现普遍适用的政府模式。冷战可能掩盖了这一事实。苏联和美国都试图说服世界，他们的制度是秩序社会的最佳方式。两国都认为他们应该把文明的礼物送给世界。虽然罗尔斯拒绝接受马克思主义和自由主义可以展示预定历史目标的信念，但他仍然回归到类似的普遍主义倾向。罗尔斯花了二十年时间思考正义，断言他的结论是任何理性的人都会得出的结论。

虽然有这种局限性，但是《正义论》可以说成为二十世纪后期最具影响力的政治理论著作。在诺贝尔奖获奖哲学家和经济学家阿马蒂亚·森等著名思想家的著作中，它仍然具有实际上是核心的影响力。[5]

局限性

罗尔斯在他后来的著作里反思了有争议的问题，即他的著作是否能普遍适用。在他的《万民法》[6]一书中，他提出了对国际正义的看法。其他学者也在争论他的理论是否可以在全球范围内应用，以及它是否适用于那些不是传统自由主义的社会。[7]

在《正义论》中，罗尔斯讨论了在国际范围内应用他的观点。

他声称他的"原初状态"的"思想实验"只能证明正义的第一原则是每个国家同等自由的权利。从这个意义上说，罗尔斯的理论是普遍的。它证明了各国应该同样自由地行使自决和自卫的观点。[8]

罗尔斯说，他的第二个正义原则——关于机会分配——并不普遍适用，因为它基于一个具有共同正义感的社群。甚至像欧盟这样一个据称基于共同的欧洲价值观和身份的机构也在这一领域面临着相当大的挑战。很难建立一个公平分配资金的系统，并决定适当的政府支出政策。这限制了，甚至可能反驳了罗尔斯的普遍正义原则理论。

或许，这些原则只适用于一个自由社会（所有成员都有相似的正义感）的国内情形。[9]

---

1. 参阅关于"秩序井然的社会"概念的介绍性讨论，涛慕思·博格和米歇尔·科什：《约翰·罗尔斯：生平与正义论》，牛津与纽约：牛津大学出版社，2007年，第137—139页。
2. 参见约翰·罗尔斯：《万民法：重新审视公共理性的思想》，坎布里奇：哈佛大学出版社，1999年。
3. G. A. 科恩：《拯救正义与平等》，坎布里奇：哈佛大学出版社，2008年，第11页。
4. 约翰·罗尔斯：《正义论（修订版）》，坎布里奇：哈佛大学贝尔纳普出版社，1999年，第10页。
5. 参见阿马蒂亚·森：《正义的理念》，坎布里奇：哈佛大学贝尔纳普出版社，2009年。
6. 罗尔斯：《万民法》。
7. 托马斯·纳格尔："全球正义问题"，《哲学与公共事务》第33卷，2005年第2

期,第 113—147 页;涛慕思·博格:《世界贫困和人权:世界性责任与改革》(第 2 版),剑桥:政体出版社,2008 年;查尔斯·贝茨:《政治理论与国际关系》(第 2 版),普林斯顿:普林斯顿大学出版社,1999 年;阿拉斯代尔·麦金太尔:《谁的正义? 理性何在?》,伦敦:达克沃斯,1988 年。
8. 罗尔斯:《正义论》,第 331—332 页。
9. 罗尔斯:《正义论》,第 497 页。

8 著作地位

要点

- 《正义论》是罗尔斯著作的学术升华。
- 在这本书中,罗尔斯发展了他早期关于社会正义的观点,超越了对概念的简单探索,发展了一个理解正义的完整系统。
- 《正义论》使罗尔斯的名字在政治哲学领域中享有盛名;他在职业生涯的后期完善了他的论点并回应了他的许多崇拜者和批评者。

定位

当约翰·罗尔斯于1971年出版《正义论》时,他已经在包括牛津和哈佛在内的世界上一些最精英的大学里学习和工作过。然而,该书是他首次以书籍形式出版的成果,并成为他发表的著作中最具现实意义和最受好评的一部。这本著作部分来自罗尔斯以前的论文和学术文章。他于1962年开始着手准备这本书。经过几次修改后,最终于1971年出版。那时,罗尔斯已经50岁,是哈佛大学哲学系主任。

《正义论》是罗尔斯早期作品的汇编和扩展。正义问题几乎是他所有内容的核心。罗尔斯的传记作者、德国出生的哲学家涛慕思·博格指出:罗尔斯对正义的终生研究最初源于他的基督教宗教精神。在罗尔斯放弃他的信仰后,变得更加有动力。罗尔斯需要找到一个合适的宗教替代品,以此作为他的社会道德的基础。[1] 书的第三部分可以看作是罗尔斯自身社会参与的反映。在学术界之外,他是各种社会正义运动的成员,反对越南战争。

1999年，罗尔斯发表了第二版《正义论》。虽然他没有放弃甚至显著地改变他在初版中的任何主要观点或哲学论点，但在序言中他承认了一些他认为特别重要或有效的批评。然后，他引导读者注意他随后的修订。罗尔斯可以被看作是一个寻求改进（而不是重新发明或抛弃）他早期思想的学者。甚至他的修订也与他对"反思均衡"的信念保持一致：几乎所有这些都与使他的定义和思想更清晰、更准确有关。[2]

> "尽管对初版有许多批评，但我仍然接受其主要框架，并捍卫其核心理论。当然，正如人们所预料的那样，我希望对有些内容做不同的处理，并做出一些重要的修改。但如果我重写《正义论》，我也不会像作者们有时说的那样，写一本完全不同的书。"
>
> ——约翰·罗尔斯：《正义论》修订版序言

整合

罗尔斯的著作非常缜密。他的整个工作可以被视为对几个关键主题的讨论：社会正义、公平、人权、社会伦理。这些主题被反复讨论，因为罗尔斯正在进行一个使它们在哲学上更连贯，更具政治意义的过程，并且他希望更具说服力。

我们可以认为《正义论》从根本上描述了罗尔斯的思想。在他随后的出版物中，他致力于两项主要任务。第一个是通过回应他的批评者澄清、重述或修改他的理论（他的第二本书，题为《政治自由主义》[3]的散文集，专注于此，正如1999年修订版的《正义论》一样）。

罗尔斯的第二个任务是发展和扩展他的理论的某些方面。虽然《正义论》主要关注的是国内正义，但罗尔斯的最终出版物《万民法》[4]则参照国际政治背景讨论了政治理论中的正义。在这里，罗尔斯详细阐述了国际正义理论，该理论在《正义论》中有简要概述。[5]他在为人权组织大赦国际*举办的公开演讲中进一步发展了这些观点。[6]罗尔斯试图评估他的想法可以应用于国际关系问题的程度。

意义

罗尔斯的著作是紧凑的、一致的，并且严格专注于他的学术研究主题：研究公正社会的理论。从方法论和概念上来说，罗尔斯的学术著作仍然是一致的，即使经过修订和修改。罗尔斯在《正义论》中定义的高度专业化的词汇影响了随后几十年的政治理论辩论，并在各种出版物中保持基本不变。

尽管《正义论》引发了许多批评和反驳，但其影响力是无可置疑的。罗尔斯改变了关于政治理论的学术辩论，他的知识和学术成就几乎不可能在质量或重要性上有所超越。

罗尔斯的工作是如此有影响力，以至于他在1999年被比尔·克林顿*总统授予国家人文奖章——这项奖章授予加深国家对人文学科理解的著作。克林顿总统在简短演讲中解释了授予约翰·罗尔斯奖章的原因，他指出了他的工作对他和他的政治发展以及他的妻子希拉里的影响。克林顿说："当希拉里和我在法学院时，我们是数百万"被罗尔斯的书感动的人之一。克林顿说，罗尔斯"帮助了整整一代美国知识分子恢复他们对民主的信仰。"[7]

1. 参见约翰·罗尔斯:"50年后的广岛",《异议》,1995年夏,第323—327页。另见涛慕思·博格和米歇尔·科什:《约翰·罗尔斯:生平与正义论》,牛津和纽约:牛津大学出版社,2007年,第18—19页。
2. 约翰·罗尔斯:《正义论(修订版)》,坎布里奇:哈佛大学贝尔纳普出版社,1999年,序言第11—16页。
3. 约翰·罗尔斯:《政治自由主义》,纽约:哥伦比亚大学出版社,1993年。
4. 约翰·罗尔斯:《万民法:重新审视公共理性的思想》,坎布里奇:哈佛大学出版社,1999年。
5. 罗尔斯在《正义论》第331—335页第58段中提到了国家法的概念,后来成为万民法。
6. 讲座发表在《约翰·罗尔斯论文集》上,塞缪尔·理查德·弗里曼编,坎布里奇:哈佛大学出版社,1999年。
7. 比尔·克林顿:《美国总统的公开文件:比尔·克林顿》,1999年,第1628—1629页。

第三部分：学术影响

9 最初反响

要点 🗝

- 罗尔斯受到政治领域左翼和右翼的一些思想家的批评,特别是在平等问题上。
- 罗尔斯承认,平等问题是他推理链中最薄弱的环节。
- 在《正义论》中表达的观点是如此引人注目,以至于它们使参与辩论的每个人的论点更加尖锐,包括批评罗尔斯的假设或目标的思想家。

批评

美国哲学家罗伯特·诺齐克仅在1971年出版约翰·罗尔斯的《正义论》几年后,发表了一篇论文,反对罗尔斯通过税收和再分配使社会更加平等的观点。[1] 社群主义*思想家的批评越来越多。社群主义者反对人类可以独立于他们所属的社会和社区发展道德观念的观点。

社群主义思想家,如苏格兰哲学家阿拉斯戴尔·麦金太尔*和加拿大哲学家查尔斯·泰勒*,批评罗尔斯理论的实质。他们批评了人类能够道德公正的观点,并认为罗尔斯优先考虑"正当"而非"善的"是有问题的。[2] 麦金太尔认为,个人的伦理观念不能被理解为可以脱离他们所属的文化和历史传统,这意味着对"正当"的东西存在普遍的人类一致的观点是非历史的,且引入歧途。[3] 同样,泰勒说,不可能从他们所发展的"社会矩阵"中抽象道德原则;换句话说,对一个社会来说,什么是正确的,不能脱离对一个人有益的东西。⁴ 罗尔斯的另一个社群主义批评者，美国哲学家迈克尔·桑德尔，挑战罗尔斯对原初状态的看法。⁵ 桑德尔认为，这是不可能的。在特定的社会和道德背景之外，个体能够具有抽象的道德理性。

左派学者也批评罗尔斯。马克思主义学者杰拉尔德·科恩认为罗尔斯的平等定义不够人人平等。根据科恩的说法，一个真正平等的正义理论无法证明罗尔斯的差异原则所承认的不平等程度。他反对罗尔斯的观点，即如果可以看出不平等有利于社会中最不利的成员，那么就应该容忍不平等。⁶

> "最严重的弱点之一是在对自由的解释中，H. L. A. 哈特在1973年的批评讨论中指出的那些缺点……初版的第二个严重缺点是它对基本善的描述……这些修正太多，以至于无法在此提及，但我认为，从初版的角度来看，它们并没有任何重要的偏离。"
>
> ——约翰·罗尔斯：《正义论》修订版序言

回应

罗尔斯在一系列不同的讲座和出版物以及《正义论》（1999）的修订版中向他的批评者发声。他对批评的回应是将任何可能削弱他理论的批评纳入他的论辩中，在他觉得批评是对的时，进行反思并调整他的观点。他还提出了对批评者的反驳，这刺激了进一步的学术辩论。

在修订版的《正义论》中，罗尔斯提及了英国哲学家哈特对他的观点的早期批评。哈特指出了罗尔斯自由概念的问题。⁷ 作为回应，罗尔斯提出了对自由论述的修正。在其他论文和讲座中，罗尔斯回答了他的社群主义的批评者。[8] 在他的散文集《政治自由主义》中，罗尔斯指出他的理论实际上是一种*政治*自由主义理论。这意味着他正在政治领域讨论道德问题。这不会干扰其他道德观念，只要这些观点是合理的并且不违反正义原则。政治自由主义不是一种总体的道德观念（与宗教不同）；相反，它是考虑到多元主义，这种政治制度可以容纳来自不同背景的人，特别是在种族或宗教方面。

澄清了这些观点后，罗尔斯坚持他理论的实质；他并没有改变他在不同社会中对正义的看法。

冲突与共识

正如我们所看到的，许多重要的批评来自社群主义思想家。特别有影响力的是哲学家迈克尔·桑德尔和查尔斯·泰勒提出的论点，即个人有综合的善的概念，这些概念影响我们的正义思想和什么是正当的。这反驳了罗尔斯的观点，在一个公正的社会中，*正当优先于善的*。

也许罗尔斯的理论最重要的发展是出版了他的著作《万民法》。此书使用他的基本正义理论作为在国际范围内讨论正义问题的基础。[9] 在这本书中，罗尔斯发展并大大改变了他在《正义论》中简要介绍过的关于国际正义的观点。然而，这些修改不能主要归功于其他学者的批评，而是由于罗尔斯自己意识到他的理论在国际政治背景下的局限性。

学者们普遍认为，对罗尔斯理论的批评不会对他的著作造成致命的打击。罗尔斯的理论仍然是政治理论领域中最有成就的学术范例。罗尔斯的批评者仍然活跃，而且确实仍然批评，但他的作品仍然是当代政治理论的重要参考，引发原创思想和辩论。

1. 参见例如罗伯特·诺齐克:《无政府状态、国家和乌托邦》,牛津布莱克威尔出版社,1974年。基于同样的理论,其他政治概念,如最低限度国家和无政府主义,已经被捍卫为尽量减少对人民消极自由干涉的方式。
2. 参见阿拉斯代尔·C.麦金太尔:《美德之后:道德理论研究》(第3版),圣母大学出版社,2007年;查尔斯·泰勒:《人类施为和语言:哲学论文(第一卷)》,剑桥大学出版社,1985年。
3. 麦金太尔:《美德之后》。
4. 泰勒:《人类施为和语言》。
5. 迈克尔·桑德尔:《自由主义与正义的界限》(第2版),剑桥:剑桥大学出版社,1998年。
6. G. A. 科恩:《拯救正义与平等》,坎布里奇:哈佛大学出版社,2008年。
7. H. L. A. 哈特:"罗尔斯论自由与优先",《芝加哥大学法律评论》第40卷,1973年第3期,第534—555页。
8. 约翰·罗尔斯:《政治自由主义》,纽约:哥伦比亚大学出版社,1993年。
9. 约翰·罗尔斯:《万民法:重新审视公共理性的理念》,坎布里奇:哈佛大学出版社,1999年。

10 后续争议

要点

- 罗尔斯的支持者将他的思想扩展到国际关系和全球正义领域。
- 学者们有时会自我认同为"罗尔斯主义者",以表达他们与罗尔斯思想的普遍一致意见。
- 《正义论》继续影响当前的政治争议;例如,罗尔斯的想法被用来讨论经济和环境问题。

应用与问题

罗尔斯的《正义论》仍然被用来讨论当前的政治和社会问题。在一个日益相互联系的世界中学者们关注罗尔斯在全球正义方面的论述。公平正义如何与全球环境问题相关? 哪种情况和原因可能决定一场正义战争? 使用无人驾驶飞机等新型军事技术会引发哪些道德问题?

罗尔斯的著作提供了一个强大的分析框架来思考这些问题的可能答案。在回应《正义论》时出现的学术著作已经探讨了许多问题。

罗尔斯的基本权利概念被批评为极简主义。他的著作主要涉及政治和公民权利,并没有涉及社会和经济等再分配原则。这种疏忽引发了一些学者的反应,他们认为政治制度有道德义务要解决全球范围内的不平等。例如,哲学家涛慕思·博格已经发展了全球再分配税[*1]的概念,并赋予了国际机构权力。政治理论家查尔斯·贝茨[2]认为有必要将经济和社会权利完全纳入普遍人权。这些想法与罗尔斯极简主义的人权理论相冲突。罗尔斯没有规定促进人权的具体行动或机构。他只是提出了一种理性思考这些问题的方法，并认为思考这些问题会推动问题的解决是合理的。

> "约翰·罗尔斯的《万民法》代表了他对如何在一个公正的世界中合理和平地生活在一起的思想的巅峰。我写这篇文章的目的部分是为了更像保皇派而非国王来表达敬意：我认为罗尔斯的正义理论能够而且应该得到延伸……结果是全球正义的概念在罗尔斯自己的术语中更加自由。"
>
> ——安德鲁·库珀：《罗尔斯全球正义：超越民族法，走向世界性的人的法律》

思想流派

罗尔斯的著作产生了一种被称为"罗尔斯思想"或"罗尔斯主义"的思想流派。在罗尔斯传记中，涛慕思·博格提供了罗尔斯最有影响力的学生名单。其中许多人是当代最具影响力的政治思想家[3]；但应该注意的是，他们经常调整、纠正或重新解释罗尔斯理论的重要组成部分，以适应他们自己的利益和论点。

当《正义论》首次出版时，全球化*——全球经济和文化的融合——以及人类生存的相互联系并不像它们在随后的几十年中那样具有相关性。这就是为什么《正义论》的国际层面是相当微不足道的。罗尔斯的思想家建立在罗尔斯的理论基础上，将其应用于全球社会和政治领域。贝茨和博格等思想家不同意罗尔斯在全球正义中的极简主义。他们的世界主义*理论——属于自由政治理论的一个分支，其特点是对普遍形式的公民身份的承诺——在公民、政治、经济和社会领域寻求对普遍人权的承认。

罗尔斯提出了一个狭义的国际正义概念；在他的著作中，自由被认为具有普遍的吸引力，平等与国内政治密切相关。然而，诸如博格这样的思想家主张将罗尔斯的正义原则扩展到普遍的领域，这催生了全球再分配正义理论。[4]

罗尔斯的工作从根本上改变了政治理论领域的争论。虽然他的理论具有很强的影响力并且塑造了许多学者的思想，但政治理论领域已经在某种程度上过于关注罗尔斯的著作；这或许可能会削弱其促进创新的能力。[5]

当代研究

认为罗尔斯对他们的思想有主要影响的学者有查尔斯·贝茨、涛慕思·博格、美国哲学家托马斯·纳格尔*、托马斯·斯坎伦*、乔舒亚·科恩、塞缪尔·弗里曼*和保罗·魏斯曼，还有爱尔兰哲学家奥诺拉·奥尼尔*。贝茨、美国哲学家玛莎·努斯鲍姆和英国政治理论家西蒙·凯尼等世界主义思想家利用他的思想来谈论全球正义问题。这场争议的大部分围绕罗尔斯在《万民法》一书中提出的国际正义观是否保证了充分的正义标准。对这场争议做出贡献的另一位重要学者是印度出生的有影响力的哲学家阿马蒂亚·森，他讨论了不平等问题和如何衡量贫困。[6]

虽然全球正义和不平等问题已在政治争议中得到广泛讨论，但其他问题，如环境保护问题和代际正义问题，仍在不断涌现。英国哲学家布赖恩·巴里*从代际问题的角度讨论了罗尔斯理论的局限性——但这是一场将继续更新的争议。在新的国内和国际政治背景下，对正义的要求将不断出现。[7]

同样，虽然正义战争的问题已有几个世纪的历史，但自2000

年以来的"新战争"对战争的道德及其规则提出了新的问题;罗尔斯没有直接探讨这些问题,也许可以通过他的理论提供的框架概念来找到答案。

---

1. 涛慕思·博格:"消除系统性贫困:全球资源红利简介",《人类发展杂志》第2卷,2001年第1期,第59—77页。
2. 查尔斯·R.贝茨:《政治理论与国际关系》(第2版),普林斯顿:普林斯顿大学出版社,1999年。
3. 托马斯·温弗里德·博格和米歇尔·科什:《约翰·罗尔斯:生平与正义论》,伦敦:牛津大学出版社,2007年,第24页。
4. 对于这一提议的版本,参见博格和"消除系统性贫困"。
5. 例如,考虑一下伯科威茨在这方面提出的批评,皮特·贝科维茨:"罗尔斯影响的模糊性",《政治观点》第4卷,2006年第1期,第121—133页。
6. 阿马蒂亚·森:《不平等之再考察》,牛津:克拉伦登出版社,1992年;《以自由看待发展》,牛津:牛津大学出版社,2001年。
7. 布赖恩·巴里:《正义理论》,亨普斯特德:哈维斯特·惠特谢夫出版社,1989年。

11 当代印迹

要点

- 虽然自《正义论》出版以来已有 40 多年的历史,但在更多的思想领域的著作中,它被引用的次数比以往任何时候都多。
- 一些学者仍然不相信罗尔斯关于平等的讨论;他们试图为平等问题建立自己的创新解决方案。
- 即使罗尔斯最严厉的批评者仍然认为他的著作是不可忽视的理论。

地位

约翰·罗尔斯的开创性著作《正义论》现在可能比写作时更有意义。

2010 年,主要政治理论家阿马蒂亚·森发表了他的著名作品《正义理念》——其中很大一部分致力于讨论罗尔斯的理论。森是哈佛大学罗尔斯的同事。他们的思想交流持续了数十年,在当代学术辩论中产生了对政治理论的一些最重要的贡献。在《正义理念》[1]中,森提出了对罗尔斯正义理论彻底和创新的批判。他对罗尔斯论点的主要批评是,它以公正社会应该依赖的完美原则来界定正义。根据森,这种"超验制度主义"(即它对制度的性质和作用所做出的假设)应该被抛弃;取而代之的应该是对现有制度及其社会影响进行评估和比较。他声称像杰里米·边沁、亚当·斯密和卡尔·马克思等思想家已经参与了这一比较过程。森称之为"以实现为中心的比较",并将自己置于这一传统中。

这种相当务实的学术辩论方法来自森的基本假设,即推理不能提供自由主义思想家所期望的普遍的和无可争议的原则。即使在"原初状态"的罗尔斯思想实验的条件下也不会发生这种情况。此外，即使理性确实有能力确定完美的正义原则，人类也不一定遵循其指令。森认为不公正仍然会发生。通过提出另一种发展正义理论的方法，森为罗尔斯的争议提供了另一种贡献。这可能引发进一步的反对观点，使政治理论领域正义的争议持续下去。

> "二十世纪西方民主国家的发展对自由主义的社会正义概念造成了越来越严重的压力。这个过程涉及的两个主要因素是与非资本主义*社会的国际竞争，以及精英和被剥夺者之间不断发生的内部冲突……鉴于这些发展，并不奇怪像约翰·罗尔斯的《正义论》这样的书可能触发相当大的争议——也许比自凯恩斯的《通论》以来社会理论中的任何其他著作都要多。"
> ——巴里·克拉克和赫伯特·金迪斯：《罗尔斯正义与经济制度》

互动

令人惊讶的是，罗尔斯的著作并非主要受到他自己公开反对的人——功利主义者和直觉主义者的挑战。这可能是因为他的书很有影响力，以至于这些思想流派已经过时了。但是，在政治领域的两极都存在着不认同罗尔斯著作的群体。

罗尔斯另一位著名批评者是美国哲学家罗伯特·诺齐克。诺齐克的作品《无政府主义、国家和乌托邦》于1974年出版，强烈地批评罗尔斯。诺齐克批评了罗尔斯的社会正义，尤其是再分配的观念。诺齐克是一个自由意志主义者*。自由意志主义的主要关注点是个人有权利采取自主行动，尽可能避免对社会的义务和纠缠。诺齐克反对通过征税和分配利益来鼓励社会平等的想法。对罗尔斯而言是社会正义和遵循差异原则，而对诺齐克只不过是国家认可的盗窃。[2]

来自相反方向的是马克思主义思想家，如哲学家杰拉尔德·科恩。像诺齐克一样，科恩批评罗尔斯关于平等的讨论，但出于相反的原因。科恩认为罗尔斯所描述的正义实际上要求完全平等。因此，罗尔斯的差异原则——如果这些不平等有益于社会，它允许不同数量的财富和地位——实际上是一种削弱其整个正义理论的方法。[3]

持续争议

围绕罗尔斯著作的大部分争议关注的是他应用他的想法的方式是否广泛，或者如何以新的方式或在新的环境中应用它。不出所料，政治理论的焦点随着政治问题的变化而变化。这至少部分地解释了为什么罗尔斯的思想现在正在经济学和环境主义等领域备受争议。

像阿马蒂亚·森和美国学者尼恩赫·谢*这样的经济思想家使用罗尔斯的正义原则来思考创造公正经济秩序所需要的东西。谢借鉴了《正义论》和罗尔斯后来出版的《万民法》，将罗尔斯的思想应用于商业道德问题。他使用罗尔斯的观点来论证跨国公司——跨国界经营的公司——有义务帮助发展中经济体的人们。他建议他们应该实施公平政策如劳工权利和环境保护。[4]

最近的环境著作，如挪威政治理论家奥朗夫·朗格勒*的著作，将罗尔斯的想法应用于环境商品。这类似于罗尔斯在《正义论》[5]中讨论经济商品和财富的方式。在这样做的过程中，朗格勒遵循查尔斯·贝茨的传统，他将罗尔斯的思想应用于全球社会正义问题。

---

1. 阿马蒂亚·森：《正义理念》，坎布里奇：哈佛大学贝尔纳普出版社，2009年。
2. 罗伯特·诺齐克："分配正义"，《哲学与公共事务》，1973年，第79—81页。
3. 对罗尔斯最相关的批判性观察见于G. A. 科恩：《拯救正义与平等》，坎布里奇：哈佛大学出版社，2008年。
4. 尼恩赫·谢："跨国公司的义务：罗尔斯的正义和援助义务"，《商业道德季刊》第14卷，2004年第4期，第643页。
5. 奥朗夫·朗格勒："可持续发展和社会正义：扩大罗尔斯全球正义框架"，《环境价值》第9卷，2000年第3期，第295—323页。

12 未来展望

要点

- 罗尔斯的《正义论》,其公平与有限平等的相关原则及其众多分析工具使其成为一部一经推出便为经典的著作。
- 对罗尔斯著作的兴趣仍然非常浓厚。许多政治思想家认为,他的作品必须在涉及其关键主题的任何讨论中得到公认。
- 对各种问题感兴趣的思想家现在使用罗尔斯关于正义的观点。这些问题包括从发展和人权到环境。

潜力

约翰·罗尔斯的开创性著作《正义论》的影响在其自身领域和相关学术背景下都是巨大的。在该书出版40多年后,政治理论家称其为该领域最显著的(如果不是最重要的)贡献之一。也许最明显的迹象表明罗尔斯的地位是由他最尖锐的批评家之一哲学家杰拉尔德·科恩授予他的[1]。科恩评论说,"西方政治哲学史上最多有两本书被认为比《正义论》更重要:柏拉图的《理想国》和霍布斯的《利维坦》。"[2]古希腊哲学家柏拉图和英国哲学家托马斯·霍布斯的作品不仅仅被视为经典。它们被视为理解政治社会和哲学的不可或缺的作品。对于一个批评家来说,把罗尔斯与这样的伟大思想家同列,就充分证明了罗尔斯作为一个具有独创性和挑战性的思想家的声誉。

道德哲学,认识论(知识研究)和经济学领域也受到罗尔斯理论的显著影响。这并不奇怪,因为他的想法深入研究了道德问题。人们和社会应该如何判断什么是道德上正确的?然而,罗尔斯本人表示，理论只适用于最基本的社会结构。³ 这使得《正义论》在政治理论及其相关领域之外的影响很难估计。

> "我的希望是公平正义在一系列深思熟虑的政治观点上似乎是合理有用的，即使不完全令人信服，从而表达了民主传统共同核心的重要组成部分。"
>
> ——约翰·罗尔斯：《正义论》修订版序言

未来方向

罗尔斯理论的复杂性意味着他的思想不断被重新诠释并应用于新的研究领域。今天，罗尔斯思想学派是最具影响力的政治理论之一。甚至那些批评过罗尔斯的思想家也要探讨他的思想以及追随罗尔斯的思想家们对其思想的发展。

罗尔斯的正义方法继续影响着其他思想家处理这一概念以及管理社会的方式。其他学科的学者也借鉴他的成果。例如，对可持续发展感兴趣的学者使用罗尔斯的论点，即以可持续的方式行事是正确的——这是道德的或公平的——无论是对于今天的人还是为了后代。

但并非所有罗尔斯的思想都在实践中完美实现。国际政治学者尚未找到一种方法来调和不同民族国家关于什么是正义的或好的观点。尽管如此，罗尔斯的著作与在国际事务中创造普遍接受的规范的必要性产生共鸣。越多人在全球范围内生活、贸易、工作、进行政治活动，就越需要对正义的含义达成共识。

小结

《正义论》启发并继续激励对社会正义观念感兴趣的许多领域

的学者。哲学家、立法者、战争抗议者、人权活动家以及众多其他专业人士受到了罗尔斯的启发和挑战。他独创的和高度开放的方法专注于创建一个最关心所有公民的社会。与许多其他政治哲学家相比，罗尔斯向读者展示了如何复制他的思想。这使他们能够自己想象哪些制度和实践最有可能实现他们愿意生活在其中的状态——即使他们处于社会阶梯的底层。

虽然写于1971年，罗尔斯的思想实验以及他从中得出的概念比以往任何时候都更有用。诸如全球化*、环境退化、就业性质的变化以及跨国公司的力量等问题，都需要人们思考正义、平等和公平。正如罗尔斯所说："正义是社会制度的第一道德，正如真理是思想体系的第一道德。"[4]

《正义论》将仍然是一部为读者提供具有挑战性的思想、哲学反思以及政治和社会灵感的著作。

---

1. G. A. 科恩：《拯救正义与平等》，坎布里奇：哈佛大学出版社，2008年。
2. 科恩：《拯救正义与平等》，第11页。
3. 路易斯·菲利普·霍奇森："为什么是基本结构？"，《加拿大哲学杂志》第42卷，2012年第3—4卷，第303—334页。
4. 罗尔斯：《正义论》，第3页。

术语表

1. **大赦国际**：一个旨在支持人权（特别是那些因政治信仰而被监禁的人）的国际组织。

2. **资本主义**：一种依靠市场来确定特定商品的供应和价格的经济制度。它假设人们是理性的行为者，根据最有益的因素做出决策。

3. **绝对命令**：在哲学家伊曼纽尔·康德的道德理论中，绝对命令认为某些道德义务由我们的本性决定为理性道德存在，且总是普遍地（绝对地）有效，命令我们依据理性标准做我们应该做的事。

4. **民权法案**：1964年的一项法律，正式禁止在美国的住房、就业、教育和其他公共环境中基于性别和种族的歧视。至关重要的是，它实施了一系列保护措施，以确保少数民族能够在公平选举中投票。

5. **民权运动**：一场从20世纪50年代开始在美国实现种族公正和平等的斗争。它的许多关键时刻发生在20世纪60年代，包括马尔科姆·X和马丁·路德·金的演讲，以及民权法案的通过。

6. **冷战（1947—1989年）**：一段美国和苏联之间的紧张时期。虽然两国从未发生过直接的军事冲突，但它们之间却进行了隐蔽和代理人的战争，以及互派间谍活动。

7. **社群主义**：一种政治理论潮流，是对自由主义政治理论兴起的反应，特别是在罗尔斯的《正义论》出版之后。社群主义者批评自由主义个人主义者的各个方面，特别是自主人类能够独立于他们自然所属的社会和社区发展道德观念的观点。

8. **宪政主义**：研究宪法，特别是成文法，但也认为每个国家或社会都受某一基本价值观的支配，所有其他法律都来自这一价值观。

9. **契约主义**：西方政治理论的一个关键分支。它基于这样一种观点，即人类通过成为他们之间假设的契约的一部分认可社会生活的条件，在这种契约中，他们就在社会中共同生活的规则和条件达成

一致。这一传统中的一些主要思想家是托马斯·霍布斯（1588—1679），约翰·洛克（1632—1704），伊曼努尔·康德（1724—1804）和让-雅克·卢梭（1712—1778）。

10. **世界主义**：自由主义政治理论的一个分支，特点是其普遍性和对普遍形式的公民身份的承诺。"世界主义"（字面意思是"世界公民"）这个词可以追溯到古典的希腊哲学，当时斯多葛哲学家提出人类实际上是世界公民的观点。

11. **民主化**：国家在组织国家机构和选举领导人方面赋予公民更多权力的过程。

12. **发展**：也称为人类发展，此领域促进缺乏经济、教育和其他自给自足和最低繁荣所需资源社会的幸福。

13. **差异原则**：罗尔斯在其正义理论中列出的第二个原则。该原则提出，只有这种分配有利于该社会中最不利的人，并且他们依附于对所有人开放的职务和职位，才能容忍在公正社会中不均等的货物分配。这一原则构成了罗尔斯正义理论的平等主义内容，并在整本书中以各种形式表述。

14. **启蒙运动**：17世纪中叶至19世纪初的一股西欧知识分子潮流，其特征是一场理性对迷信的运动，及其教育和知识可以改善人类状况的信念。

15. **全球再分配税**：涛慕思·博格提出的一种理论税，它可以让世界变得更公正，将资源转移到以前处于不利或贫困状态的国家和社会。

16. **全球化**：政治、文化和经济结构在世界范围内变得更加统一的过程。由于技术、旅游、国际商务和全球媒体的发展，许多人认为全球化正变得越来越明显。

17. **广岛**：与长崎一样，是战争史上两枚原子弹袭击地之一；都是日本的城市。使用原子弹被视为迫使日本投降并结束太平洋地区第二次世界大战的必要罪恶。学者和社会继续激烈地辩论该行为的伦理和必要性。

18. **大屠杀**：这一事件被认为是人类历史的一个低点。在第二次世界大战期间，纳粹及其合作者以系统化和高度组织化的方式杀害了1 100多万人。这些人中约有600万人仅仅因为是犹太人而被杀。其他被指向灭绝的群体包括罗姆人（"吉卜赛人"）、同性恋者以及患有身心残疾的人。

19. **人权**：一般被认为具有普遍性，这些权利仅因人道而存在。存在各种法律和条约来促进和保护这些权利，包括成为公民的权利、参与政府的自由、公平审判等等。

20. **工业时代**：从18世纪中期开始直到20世纪的一段时期，其间机器、市场、大规模生产和其他技术迅速发展，从根本上改变了日常生活和社会。

21. **直觉主义**：根据罗尔斯的观点，"把它作为一种含有一组不能再追溯的最初原则的理论，那些最初原则是必须通过咨询我们自己来衡量，在我们深思熟虑的判断中确定哪些平衡是最正义的。"在直觉主义中，没有优先权规则或者方法来平衡一种正义原则与另一种原则之间的冲突；这种原则之间的平衡通过直觉来完成。

22. **公平正义**：根据这一概念，定义正义的原则是在任何人都认为公平的程序的基础上达成的，因为它们导致的结论被任何理性的人认为是合法的，独立于任何偶然特性。为了达到公平的条件，罗尔斯制定了原初状态的思想实验及其相关概念。

23. **克雷山脊**：罗尔斯在第二次世界大战中战斗过的一处菲律宾战场。正是在这里，他听到一位牧师讲道，说上帝指示盟军的子弹射击日本人。这导致罗尔斯深深质疑并最终抛弃他的基督教信仰。

24. **妇女选民联盟**：美国的一个组织，旨在鼓励妇女在国家的公民结构中获得具有影响力的职位。它是在美国妇女获准投票后不久成立的。

25. **自由主义**：西方文化最相关的政治理论之一，在十八世纪的启蒙运动中有其基础，主要与伊曼努尔·康德和约翰·洛克等思想家有关。其历史基础与自由公民的个人解放有关，特别是在法国大革命（1789年）——法国政治改革的一个时期，其中君主制被推翻，政府民主化。它的核心问题是政治机构的正当性，它保护个人自由免

受其他人,特别是政治机构和领导人的干涉。

26. **自由意志主义**:自由主义政治理论的一个子类别,它非常关注个人自由原则,特别是消极自由的原则,即一个人免受外部干涉的自由。自由主义思想的一个关键要素是个人对财产的不可剥夺的权利,罗伯特·诺齐克等自由主义者认为这些权利具有根本重要性;因此,他们批评分配正义的形式(为确保社会正义而分配财富)。

27. **纳粹(国家社会党)**:由阿道夫·希特勒领导的一个极右翼政党,从1933年到1945年统治德国。他们信仰雅利安人(日耳曼人)种族优越性,并对大屠杀中系统地杀害超过1 100万人负有罪责。他们特别反对犹太人、残疾人、同性恋者和罗姆吉卜赛人。

28. **原初状态**:原初状态是罗尔斯提出的一个思想实验,用于证明他的正义理论所确立的两个原则。思想实验从问题开始:如果一个理性的人有一块空白的画布来创造一个新的社会,他们希望社会实现什么?他们怎样才能最好地创造一个符合这些目标的社会?

29. **多元主义**:一种政治制度,可以容纳来自不同背景的人,特别是在种族或宗教方面。它旨在为所有公民提供平等权利,并确保个人可以根据自己的良心自由行事,同时促进这些群体之间的社会和谐。

30. **政治哲学**:哲学的一个分支,特别关注发展关于人类社会生活的理论以及规范它们的准则和制度。政治的哲学思辨是最古老的。在西方传统中,政治哲学可以追溯到古希腊哲学家柏拉图和亚里士多德。

31. **心理学**:研究人类思维及其如何影响人类的信仰、行为和决策。

32. **反思均衡**:这一概念描述了人们通过从其综合原则来回反复评估,然后达到平衡点来发展其认为的正义信念的方式。

33. **社会契约**:社会创造一个国家并放弃一些个人自由以换取安全和保护预定政治权利的观念。

34. **苏联**:苏维埃社会主义共和国联盟(苏联),1922年至1991年间由若干个加盟共和国组成。

35. **自然状态**:在没有政府干预的情况下,人类社会将处于自然状态的一种想象的表现。霍布斯著名的观点认为这将是暴力的和可怕的；像卢梭这样的思想家认为人们天生是和平的。

36. **目的论**：一种对历史有预定义目的或目标的知识观。

37. **思想实验**：哲学家用来创造一种假想情境的工具，这种假想情境允许他们证明某一特定观点是合乎逻辑的，或者某个结论可能出现在给定的一组情境中。例子包括霍布斯的"自然状态"和罗尔斯的"原初状态"。

38. **宽容**：一种政治价值观，认为社会应该接受不会对其他个人造成重大伤害的异见。

39. **功利主义**：一种理论，根据这种理论，效用和幸福应该成为道德决策判断的主要标准，在思考社会时，这些应该以综合的方式加以考虑，从而证明可以最大限度地发挥集体效用但不利于个人权利和福利的政策。

40. **无知之幕**：一种想象的条件，在这种条件下，在原初状态下的人做出决定和思考正义，而不知道他们的社会状况，如社会地位或阶级；他们的天赋，如智力、力量或能力；或他们个人的道德偏好。

41. **越南战争**：1955年至1975年间发生的一场冷战冲突。它被认为是当代美国历史上最具争议的事件之一，深刻地影响了美国的政治辩论。

42. **第二次世界大战**：1939年至1945年间发生的一场冲突几乎涉及地球上的每个主要国家。同盟国（美国，英国，法国，苏联和其他国家）和轴心国（德国，意大利和日本及其盟友）之间交战，它被视为自由与暴政之间的一次重大的道德斗争，包括像大屠杀这样的影响深远的事件。

人名表

1. **布赖恩·巴里**（1933—2009）：英国哲学家，曾在伦敦经济学院和哥伦比亚大学任教。尽管与罗尔斯是朋友，但他在备受推崇的著作《自由公正批判》（1972）中批评了罗尔斯的著作。

2. **查尔斯·贝茨**（1949年生）：美国政治理论家，他写了几篇关于人权和全球正义问题的研究。他最具影响力的作品之一是《政治理论与国际关系》，书中他提出了一个世界性的政治理论。

3. **杰里米·边沁**（1743—1832）：功利主义最著名的思想家。在他去世后的100多年里，他的箴言，即社会应该努力实现"最多数人的最大利益"，在政治和哲学运动中具有很大的影响力。他活跃于许多社会领域，包括监狱改革、教育和福利。

4. **以赛亚·伯林**（1909—1997）：英语世界和其他地方自由主义思想的杰出人物。他最有名的是区分消极和积极自由，以及此领域的其他贡献。

5. **比尔·克林顿**（1946年生）：美国第四十二任总统。他对政府和社会公正的态度使他对罗尔斯的许多目标抱有同情心。

6. **杰拉尔德·科恩**（1941—2009）：颇有影响的马克思主义哲学家，他是从社会主义视角批判自由主义政治理论的几部作品的作者。他的著作广泛，但对罗尔斯的一些最重要的相关批判性观点可以在《拯救正义和平等》中找到（2008）。

7. **塞缪尔·弗里曼**：宾夕法尼亚大学的教授，著有多部作品，其中包括对罗尔斯哲学著作最受欢迎的评论：《罗尔斯》（2007）。

8. **斯图尔特·汉普希尔**（1914—2004）：颇具影响力的哲学家和政治思想家，他的著作颇丰，比如他的斯宾诺莎研究，以及他在《思想和行动》和《正义是冲突》中表达的反理性主义的公共伦理观。

9. **乔纳森·哈里森**（1924—2014）：在许多大学教过书的英国哲学家。

以著作《我们对正确和错误的认识》而闻名。

10. 亨利·罗伊·福布斯·哈罗德（1900—1978）：英国经济学家，为回应经济自由主义，他创造了许多新颖的理论。他还因其经济学家约翰·梅纳德·凯恩斯的传记而闻名。

11. 赫伯特·莱昂内尔·阿道弗斯·哈特（1907—1992）：牛津颇具影响力的法律哲学家，之后在伦敦政治经济学院和其他主要的学术中心。他是对罗尔斯理论最早回应的作者之一。

12. 托马斯·霍布斯（1588—1679）：英国哲学家，他的主要著作《利维坦》，成功地运用了"自然状态"的思想实验，即人们生活在没有国家的状态下，来论证这种状况对社会来说是最糟糕的。相反，他主张建立一种社会契约，在这种契约中，生活在完全自由中的人们为了获得秩序和安全，愿意将部分自由让渡给主权国家。

13. 尼恩赫·谢：哈佛商学院工商管理系副教授。他的著作讨论诸如营利性公司是否能对社会有益的问题。

14. 大卫·休谟（1711—1776）：苏格兰启蒙运动中最重要的哲学家之一。他认为，人们应该把道德建立在他们行动对自己和社会获得快乐或利益的有用性或效用上。因此，他是功利主义政治哲学学派的奠基人。

15. 林登·约翰逊（1908—1973）：美国第三十六任总统。在肯尼迪总统被暗杀后，他上台执政，并继续前任的许多政策，包括大大扩展了越南战争，以及扩大了少数民族的民权。

16. 伊曼纽尔·康德（1724 1804）：西方现代哲学思想的奠基人之一，以大量重要作品著称，是启蒙运动的典型代表。他是理性的有力拥护者，主张建立共和政府，提倡个人政治权利。

17. 奥朗夫·朗格勒：挪威斯塔万格大学的教授。他研究可持续发展、企业社会责任、政治理论、全球化，以及许多罗尔斯关注的其他主题。

18. 约翰·洛克（1632—1704）：是英语世界和启蒙运动中最有影响力的思想家之一，他以若干思想贡献而闻名，包括《政府论》（1689）。

19. 阿拉斯代尔·麦金太尔（1929年生）：哲学家，尤其以其明确的社群主义立场而闻名，在《后美德》中呈现，在随后的作品中进一步发展。

20. 诺曼·马尔科姆（1911—1990）：美国哲学家。在剑桥大学期间和路德维希·维特根斯坦一起工作。

21. 托马斯·纳格尔（1937年生）：纽约大学颇具影响力的政治哲学家，他的一些政治理论和哲学出版物闻名于世，尤其是对还原论的批判。

22. 奥诺拉·奥尼尔（1941年生）：有影响力的康德哲学家，也是上议院议员和剑桥大学的教授。

23. 罗伯特·诺齐克（1933—2002）：重要的政治理论家，主要与自由主义自由派的分支有关。他是对罗尔斯理论进行有争议批评的作者，尤其是批评社会正义原则和再分配原则。

24. 柏拉图（公元前429—前347）：历史上最有影响和最著名的哲学家之一。他的著作《理想国》自古代以来一直影响着历代政治思想家。他最重要的政治观点是，可以想象出一个能够推进预定义的"美好生活"的理想状态。

25. 涛慕思·博格（1953年生）：哥伦比亚大学政治学教授，也是罗尔斯最年轻的学生之一。他以全球正义理论著称，倡导全球再分配原则。

26. 让–雅克·卢梭（1712—1778）：启蒙运动的主要思想家，也是法国大革命的灵感源泉。他最相关的政治理论是关于社会契约的思想。

27. 迈克尔·桑德尔（1953年生）美国哈佛大学的政治哲学家，他以批评罗尔斯正义论的著作《自由主义和正义局限性》（1998）而闻名。最近，他因为一门关于正义的创新课程而受到欢迎，该课程在媒体上广为宣传，而且可以在网上找到。

28. 托马斯·斯坎伦（1940年生）：哈佛大学阿尔福德自然宗教、道德哲学和公民政体教授，他是道德和政治哲学领域的主要学者之一，尽管他最初学的是数学。他最具影响力的著作有《宽容的困难：政治哲学论文》（2003）和《我们彼此欠对方什么》（1998）。

29. **阿马蒂亚·森**（1933年生）：哲学家和经济学家，诺贝尔奖获得者，他广泛发表了许多议题，经常在哲学和经济学的十字路口。他被称为人类发展理念和"能力方法"的创始人，这一理念随后对联合国的贫困评估产生了影响。他最近的著作之一是一篇关于正义的综合论述，其中他提出了几个批评罗尔斯理论的论点。

30. **朱迪思·什克拉**（1923—1992）：哈佛大学的政治理论家。在她的著作中，她讨论了不公正、政治罪恶和"恐惧的自由主义"。

31. **亨利·西季威克**（1838—1900）：功利主义传统的英国哲学家。他的作品常常被认为是最深刻地发展了早期边沁思想，他与边沁一样都认为社会必须努力提供"最多数人的最大利益"。

32. **亚当·斯密**（1723—1790）：苏格兰哲学家，或许是现代经济学之父。他最著名的作品《国富论》将市场称为"看不见的手"，这有助于确保商品在社会中尽可能有效地分配。他的著作是许多关于国家、商业和公民之间关系的政治自由概念的中心。

33. **查尔斯·泰勒**（1931年生）：当代最有影响的哲学家之一，尤其以论黑格尔的作品而闻名。他对自由主义政治理论的批评参见《人类施为和语言：哲学论文（第一卷）》（1985）。

34. **保罗·魏斯曼**：圣母大学政治哲学教授。他曾在罗尔斯和施克拉尔的指导下在哈佛学习，并著有多本关于政治理论，特别是罗尔斯政治自由主义的出版物。

35. **路德维希·维特根斯坦**（1889—1951）：奥地利哲学家，他对语言在人类思想中的作用、可能性及其局限性特别感兴趣。

WAYS IN TO THE TEXT

KEY POINTS

- John Rawls (1921–2002) was one of the twentieth century's most influential American philosophers.

- Rawls served in the US military during World War II.* This experience led him to write extensively about issues related to justice and society.

- *A Theory of Justice* argues that societies should pursue "justice as fairness."* He encouraged people to imagine a theoretical society that would be perceived as fair by all social classes.

Who Was John Rawls?

John Rawls, the author of *A Theory of Justice* (1971), was born in 1921 in Baltimore, Maryland to an upper-middle-class Christian family. His father was a well-known lawyer and his mother was the local president of the League of Women Voters* (an organization with a largely progressive political agenda, originally founded to help women to claim a more active role in civic life).

As an undergraduate at Princeton University, Rawls was exposed to the ideas of the American philosopher Norman Malcolm.* Malcolm had been a pupil of the Austrian philosopher Ludwig Wittgenstein,* who was fascinated by the role that language plays in the way we think. This idea would feed into Rawls's later academic interest in the way societies define what they mean by the term "justice."

Rawls's Princeton years were characterized by a deeply religious approach to political philosophy.* He considered studying theology and entering the priesthood. But when Rawls was 20, the

United States entered World War II. Two years later, Rawls was on active duty in the Pacific. His military experiences between 1943 and 1946 led him to reject his faith and to seek an alternative means of conceptualizing a good, or just, society.[1] Choosing political philosophy as the best means of realizing this goal, Rawls became an academic. He worked at the Massachusetts Institute of Technology (MIT) and Cornell University, before accepting a position at Harvard University in 1962.

In the decades before his death in 2002, John Rawls became one of the most influential and frequently cited political thinkers of his generation. His first book, *A Theory of Justice*, was published in 1971. This highly regarded work, inspiring debate, criticism, and widespread admiration, established his reputation as a political philosopher.

What Does *A Theory of Justice* Say?

John Rawls's aim in *A Theory of Justice* is to develop a new way for people to think about justice. He wants to offer an alternative to the ideas of utilitarian* philosophy. Utilitarianism argues that the morality of an action should be judged according to its consequences; a "virtuous" action achieves the greatest good for the greatest number of people. Utilitarian ideas were very popular at the time when Rawls was writing *A Theory of Justice*, but Rawls opposed them. He argues that utilitarianism ignores the wellbeing of the individual, considering only an action's benefit to the majority. This, says Rawls, opens the door to abuse and suffering.

To replace utilitarianism, Rawls revives the tradition of the social contract.* A key idea in the liberal* political tradition, with its emphasis on the importance of individual liberty, this is the idea that society is based on an implicit contract between the state and each citizen of that state. The agreement is that the individual will give up some of their natural freedoms (essentially, the freedom to do whatever they like, whenever they like), while, in exchange, the state will create a society that protects the individual.

Rawls's picture of society is a group composed of free and rational individuals with a sense of justice. This is an underlying assumption of his work. He argues that the members of this society—defined as "a cooperative venture for mutual advantage"[2]—would all agree on the principles that should underpin a just society. Rawls defines justice as fairness; for him, justice should rely on conditions and procedures that everyone regards as fair.[3] He is interested in justice as the foundation for the "basic structure" of society: core values embodied in core institutions.

Rawls argues that a truly just society is one that would be considered just by all of its members, regardless of their social class or religious or moral beliefs. As it is hard for any individual to imagine what a just society would look like from a perspective other than their own, Rawls provides tools (thought experiments*) to help his readers make this empathetic leap.[4] He also provides other ideas to help everyone reflect on social justice and what it means. These ideas include a concept that Rawls call "reflective equilibrium"*—the idea that people develop their understanding of justice by questioning and reevaluating until they reach a point of equilibrium.⁵

Rawls called another innovative concept the "difference principle."* He argues that unequal wealth can be tolerated in a just society if this inequality is beneficial to its least advantaged people; it may be socially beneficial, for example, to incentivize someone with the right abilities to spend time training to become a surgeon, as the work they would do would benefit society. But Rawls qualifies this argument by saying that the means of earning unequal wealth should come from jobs that are open to anyone on the basis of merit.⁶

The importance of Rawls's method lies in its claim to religious and cultural neutrality: all members of society should believe their society is fair. Rawls's unique approach sees people as inherently equal in worth, but recognizes that people have unequal abilities. Some people can contribute more to the good of society than others. And, finally, inequality may exist—even in a just society.

Why Does *A Theory of Justice* Matter?

Written in the tradition of liberal political theory, Rawls's work emphasizes the idea of universal human rights* and the importance of every individual human being. The key themes of *A Theory of Justice* are central pillars of the liberal tradition. They include justice, individual equality, liberty, and the importance of reason and public reasoning. And the political question he asks is a recurring one: how can people live the best life possible in a society that is best able to give all people a good life?

Some of the assumptions that Rawls makes, however, limit how his work is applied. *A Theory of Justice* was published in 1971. In the following decades, demands for justice became increasingly global in character, highlighting how deeply Rawls's theory was rooted in the Western liberal tradition. Rawls's theory of justice aims to be universal. He claims it can be universally derived and universally applied. But it is not well suited to discussing justice in international relations. Global poverty, just war, and tolerance are at the top of the global political agenda. While there is also debate about the principles that should regulate a just international society and what moral obligations people have towards those in other countries, these are issues only briefly addressed in Rawls's theory of justice. His work is primarily concerned with domestic democratic social institutions such as the legal system—but these institutions are less developed in international relations. There is also less agreement about how to share power in these contexts.

Despite the limitations to Rawls's approach, *A Theory of Justice* creates many new ideas that are still helpful for thinking about politics. More than 40 years after the text was published, Rawls's work is repeatedly referred to in discussions on a whole range of issues: from human rights, democratization,* and toleration,* to development,* pluralism,* and constitutionalism* and democratization.*

Rawls's theory provoked an extensive debate when it was published. That debate is still ongoing. But even those who oppose his ideas applaud his work; the American philosopher Michael

Sandel,* a critic of Rawls's thought, for example, says that *A Theory of Justice* is "deservedly celebrated."[7]

---

1. Eric Gregory, "Before the Original Position: The Neo-Orthodox Theology of the Young John Rawls," *Journal of Religious Ethics* 35, no. 2 (2007): 195–6.
2. John Rawls, *A Theory of Justice* (Cambridge, MA: Belknap Press of Harvard University Press, 1999), 4.
3. Among Rawls's first important publications preceding his theory is his article "Justice as Fairness," *The Philosophical Review* 67, no. 2 (1958).
4. See Rawls, *A Theory of Justice*, 118–22.
5. Rawls, *A Theory of Justice*, 17–19.
6. Rawls, *A Theory of Justice*, 72.
7. Michael J. Sandel, *Liberalism and the Limits of Justice*, 2nd ed. (Cambridge: Cambridge University Press, 1998), ix.

SECTION 1
INFLUENCES

MODULE 1
THE AUTHOR AND THE HISTORICAL CONTEXT

KEY POINTS

* John Rawls's seminal work *A Theory of Justice* is one of the most influential works of political philosophy* in the last 50 years.
* In childhood, Rawls was affected by the death of two of his brothers; his exposure to his mother's work on women's rights; and his friendships with children from poor or minority backgrounds.
* Rawls's experiences in World War II* precipitated his interest in the concept of justice.

Why Read This Text?

John Rawls's book *A Theory of Justice* was first published in 1971. It created a new school of political philosophy, Rawlsianism, and led to a flurry of scholarly thinking about justice and what this term means. Rawls's ideas and methodology sparked continuing discussions.

One reason Rawls's work is considered so important is that it offers an alternative to the philosophy of utilitarianism.* Utilitarianism looks at justice from the standpoint of society as a whole: its supporters argue that decisions should be made by considering which outcome would provide the greatest good for the greatest number of people. This approach looks at justice in the context of collective social benefit, but ignores the needs of the individual. In contrast, Rawls explores justice from the standpoint of the individual. For Rawls, justice requires that every person be treated "fairly": enjoying basic living standards and being given opportunities to move up in society.

It is hard to find a work of political theory after 1971 that does not engage with his work. *A Theory of Justice* has been published in two editions and is available in over 20 languages. Rawls argues that his ideas can be applied universally, in any time and any place. The number of translations supports this argument, as scholars from many different states, political systems, and religious traditions continue to read and address his work.

> "I have often wondered why my religious beliefs changed, particularly during the war. I started out as a believing orthodox Episcopalian Christian, and abandoned it entirely by June of 1945 ... Three incidents stand out in my memory: Kilei Ridge,* Deacon's death, hearing and thinking about the Holocaust.*"[1]
>
> —— John Rawls, "On My Religion"

Author's Life

Born in 1921 in the US city of Baltimore, Maryland, Rawls was from an upper-middle-class family. Both of his parents were practicing Christians and were active in politics. His father was a member of the Democratic Party and participated in local government and politics, and his mother was active in the local women's rights movement. But tragedy struck the family. As a child Rawls lost two younger brothers to illnesses—diphtheria and pneumonia—that they contracted from him. Sadly, these deaths occurred within a year of each other; they left Rawls with the lasting impression that life was both short and inherently unfair.²

Rawls attended faith-based schools, where he achieved excellent marks and as a young man he considered joining the priesthood and pursuing theological studies; he eventually decided to study philosophy and public ethics. After receiving his undergraduate degree from Princeton University, he joined the US Army in 1943 and fought in World War II, before returning to Princeton to complete his PhD. This was followed by a Fulbright Fellowship to Oxford University, where he met innovative thinkers such as H. L. A. Hart,* an influential philosopher of law, the liberal* philosopher Isaiah Berlin,* and the political philosopher Stuart Hampshire.*³ These scholars played a central role in the debates over political theory in the 1950s and were key influences for Rawls.⁴

His thinking was also shaped by world events of the time. At the end of World War II Rawls had been deployed in Japan. He was deeply affected by the nuclear bombardment of Hiroshima,* the first use of nuclear weapons in warfare, as well as by the Holocaust* (in the course of which the Nazis* murdered some 11 million European people, the greater part of whom were Jewish), and later by the ongoing American war in Vietnam,* which Rawls actively opposed.⁵

Author's Background

In 1971, when *A Theory of Justice* was first published, American society was experiencing rapid change; with this came violent clashes between its different social groups. Only a few years earlier the country had witnessed the flowering of the civil rights movement,* a social movement that successfully brought the suffering of America's racial minorities to the forefront of national consciousness. Internationally, the country was preoccupied with the Vietnam War. The conflict, in which the United States fought on behalf of South Vietnam against communist* North Vietnam, was the first to be broadcast on television; for the first time the American public was exposed to the violent reality of war. By the late 1960s, the conflict had divided society; many questioned the United States' ideas about justice and society's sense of fairness was shaken to the core—something evident in *A Theory of Justice*.

But what is also present is the awareness of what people can achieve when they work together towards a common goal. The 1960s, as well as being a decade of great upheaval, was also a time of great social achievements and idealism. In 1965, President Lyndon B. Johnson* signed the Civil Rights Act* into law. For the first time, all citizens were promised equal opportunities: people could vote, do business, and go to school without suffering racial discrimination. Four years later, in July 1969, the Apollo moon landings took place. The Americans were achieving things that had been thought impossible a decade earlier.

A Theory of Justice is of its time. Rawls questions fundamental assumptions about goodness and justice while believing that, through cooperation, it is possible to achieve them.

1. Deacon was a friend of Rawls who also fought in World War II.
2. Thomas Winfried Pogge and Michelle Kosch, *John Rawls: His Life and Theory of Justice* (London: Oxford University Press, 2007), 5.
3. Pogge and Kosch, *John Rawls*, 16.
4. For example, Rawls refers to Hart when proposing a distinction between the concept of justice and the various conceptions of justice that may recur among different persons: John Rawls, *A Theory of Justice*, rev. ed. (Cambridge, MA: Belknap Press of Harvard University Press, 1999), 5. More generally, Hart's theory is used by Rawls to define several key concepts of its theory. Equally, Berlin is used as a reference for the concept of liberty and the debate regarding its definitions: Rawls, *A Theory of Justice*, 177.
5. Later he would publish an article in which he argued against the use of indiscriminate weapons against civilians in Hiroshima and Tokyo. See John Rawls, "50 Years After Hiroshima," *Dissent* (summer 1995): 323–7.

MODULE 2
ACADEMIC CONTEXT

KEY POINTS

* Political theory is concerned with the ideas that form the foundation of any society. Political theorists usually try to imagine how to create a society that helps people live the "good life."

* Major schools of political theory include utilitarianism,* which seeks the greatest good for the greatest number of people, liberalism,* which seeks the greatest good for individuals, and contractarianism,* according to which individual people make a contract with the state in exchange for state provision of the means to a "good life."

* Rawls works in the liberal and contractarian traditions.

The Work in its Context

When John Rawls published *A Theory of Justice* in 1971 the academic field of political theory was facing a severe challenge. International relations were then defined by the Cold War,* a long period of tension between the United States and the Soviet Union* and nations aligned to each, dividing the capitalist* world from the communist world; across the world, states felt compelled to choose a side in this war of ideologies. Both camps believed that they knew the right way to order society. Both argued their case on the grounds of utilitarian philosophy, arguing that their system would achieve the best possible outcomes for the greatest number of people—although some people would, inevitably, not benefit.

But Rawls wanted a political theory that would create good social outcomes *without* harm to individuals. He makes this clear when he says:"Just as each person must decide by rational reflection what constitutes his good ... so a group of persons must decide once and for all what is to count among them as just and unjust."¹

In order to find a path between the extremes of existing political ideas, Rawls turns to the idea of the social contract,* found in the works of thinkers like the English philosopher John Locke* and the Swiss-born philosopher Jean-Jacques Rousseau.* The social contract is an implicit agreement of cooperation between individuals in order to create a mutually beneficial society. But, in the tradition of the German philosopher Immanuel Kant,* Rawls adds a moral and ethical dimension to this. His starting point is the individual's rational desire to have a just and fair life within society.² In *A Theory of Justice* he devises a system that societies can use to decide what is just. Rawls argues that this system can be applied to any society at any time.

> "My aim is to present a conception of justice which generalizes and carries to a higher level of abstraction the familiar theory of the social contract as found, say, in Locke, Rousseau, and Kant."
>
> —— John Rawls, *A Theory of Justice*

Overview of the Field

Rawls frequently refers to Kant, a deeply influential thinker notable for his ethical works such as *The Metaphysics of Morals* (1797). In it, Kant uses hypothetical situations to show how (rational) people can construct moral ideas that can be accepted throughout society. Rawls tends to agree with Kant that rational people are "autonomous moral agents"—that is, individuals free to think about good and bad in their own terms. Rawls also uses one of Kant's key methodologies: he puts his reader in an imagined situation and asks them—from that theoretical perspective—to describe what it means for a state to be just, fair and good.[3]

Rawls explicitly says that *A Theory of Justice* tries to offer an alternative to the utilitarian views of political theory. In the introduction to his book he argues that utilitarianism became popular largely because of the brilliance of the people who first proposed it. Rawls says that the British philosophers David Hume,* Adam Smith,* and Jeremy Bentham* were all "social theorists and economists of the first rank." But he also argues that their moral theories lacked clarity. There are many cases where it is hard to reconcile morality with a strict version of social utility.

For example: following Bentham, a state facing a lack of food or money might decide to let the weakest or least productive members of society die. That would help the state provide resources to people who can actively contribute to that society. But Rawls says that most people would rebel against the idea of sacrificing the old and the sick. Most societies give these groups special attention and consideration. Rawls's stated aim in *A Theory of Justice* is to create a "workable and systematic moral conception to oppose [utilitarianism]."[4]

Academic Influences

John Rawls is very open about the people and philosophies that influenced his work. His aims are to provide a definition of justice and, through that, to help people create just societies. These aims have been shared by thinkers throughout history. Indeed, Rawls writes that the "leading ideas are classical and well known." Locke, working in the seventeenth century, discusses the idea of a contract existing between individuals and the state. He argues that people enter into this contract with the understanding that the state will provide them with the ability to secure "life, liberty, and Estate."[5] Locke's thinking was complemented by the ideas of Rousseau, who views people as born free, but enslaved by society. Society, Rousseau argues, does not allow individuals to govern themselves or to have their own moral values.

Kant provides the last link in this chain. He argues that people should not be seen as the means to an end, but as an end in themselves—an idea he calls the categorical imperative.* For Kant, this approach provides a foundation from which people can think rationally about how they would wish to be treated by others. He is interested in how the dignity of each individual human being may be preserved.

These philosophers had a profound influence on Rawls's thought. But Rawls was also part of a vibrant intellectual community at both Oxford and Harvard and he mentions a number of his contemporaries who influenced his ideas. These individuals include well-known scholars like the Indian-born philosopher Amartya Sen,* the American philosopher Robert Nozick,* and the Latvian-born political theorist Judith Shklar.*[6] Although Nozick criticized Rawls's ideas, Rawls acknowledged that he found these criticisms useful. In contrast, Sen and Shklar both use some of Rawls's ideas in their own works.[7]

---

1. John Rawls, *A Theory of Justice*, rev. ed. (Cambridge, MA: Belknap Press of Harvard University Press, 1999), 10–11.
2. Rawls, *A Theory of Justice*, 10–12. See also his earlier work on "Justice as Fairness," *The Philosophical Review* 67, no. 2 (1958): 164–94.
3. Rawls, *A Theory of Justice*, 10–11.
4. Rawls, *A Theory of Justice*, xviii.
5. John Locke, *Two Treatises of Government*, trans. Peter Laslett (Cambridge: Cambridge University Press, 1988), 323.
6. Rawls, *A Theory of Justice*, xxi.
7. See Amartya Sen, *On Economic Inequality* (Oxford: Oxford University Press, 1973); Robert Nozick, "Distributive Justice," *Philosophy & Public Affairs* (1973): 45–126; Judith Shklar, "Giving Injustice Its Due," *Yale Law Journal* (1989): 1135–51.

MODULE 3
THE PROBLEM

KEY POINTS

- In *A Theory of Justice* John Rawls seeks to define justice and to provide society with tools that will help it to become more just.
- At the time when *A Theory of Justice* was being written, the most popular vision of justice was utilitarian:* justice, that is, was considered a question of achieving good outcomes for the greatest number of people.
- Seeking to create a theory of justice that could apply to any group of people at any time or place, Rawls rejected utilitarianism as it did not protect the rights of the individual.

Core Question

The central question asked by John Rawls in *A Theory of Justice* is: what principles should a just society be founded on? In the text Rawls justifies the importance of this question. Any society is based on shared ideas. What should be the foundation of these ideas? Rawls's answer is: truth. How can truth be protected and embodied within social institutions? His answer is: through justice. This analogy between truth in philosophy and justice in social institutions is how Rawls justifies the central question of his inquiry. Justice (that upholds truth) is the fundamental social virtue of societies. It is, therefore, a legitimate object of inquiry for thinkers committed to making societies better.[1]

When Rawls was writing, utilitarian thought was dominant in the field of political philosophy.* Utilitarianism argues that justice is served when a system achieves a desired good for society as a whole. While this argument ignores individuals, it is equally true that completely individualistic theories do not promote equality or fairness.

Rawls takes a novel approach to social contract* theory to solve this problem. He says that each person in a state is an equal citizen. Each person can think about what it means for a state to provide equal opportunity and fairness. Instead, he says that all citizens should have equal liberty (equal freedom under the law) and equality of opportunity. This means that although some people will achieve more than others, this will happen in a fair—that is, just—way.

> "Now as far as possible the basic structure should be appraised from the position of equal citizenship. This position is defined by the rights and liberties required by the principle of equal liberty and the principle of fair equality of opportunity. When the two principles are satisfied, all are equal citizens, and so everyone holds this position."
> —— John Rawls, *A Theory of Justice*

The Participants

When Rawls wrote *A Theory of Justice*, most political theorists were using a utilitarian approach to justice (an approach founded on the assumption that any given political system should be judged on its ability to create good outcomes for as many people as possible). The English philosopher Jonathan Harrison* wrote, for example, that the universal duty to be just requires a universally applicable theory that can only be found in utilitarianism. Several other writers, among them the English economist R. F. Harrod,* were trying to revise classical utilitarianism to include modern social science, economics, and a more nuanced moral system. Similarly, the English philosopher Henry Sidgwick* sought to demonstrate that utilitarianism was a moral theory that could be applied to questions of economic and social justice.[2]

While most of these thinkers were aware that utilitarianism could be used to justify atrocities in the name of the common good, they saw it as the best way to create socially beneficial political systems nonetheless. Rather than trying to produce an alternative political theory, they tried to find ways of dealing with the moral dilemmas that utilitarianism created. A concern with morality had always been central to utilitarian thinkers. The British philosophers David Hume* and Jeremy Bentham,* the main proponents of this school of thought, explicitly mention morality in the titles of their works. Hume wrote *An Enquiry Concerning the Principles of Morals* (1751), while Bentham wrote *The Principles of Morals and Legislation* (1789).[3]

The Contemporary Debate

In *A Theory of Justice*, Rawls argues against utilitarian ideas and what he calls "intuitionism."* By this, he means that a society based on utilitarianism relies on human intuition to know when it is about to cross a moral or ethical boundary that should not be violated. Rawls says this view is "not irrational; and there is no assurance that we can do better. But this is no reason not to try."⁴

Rawls points out that intuitionism means that people rely on their principles to ascertain whether a boundary is about to be violated. But intuitionism does not provide any method or rules to decide which principles are the most important. This means that it is quite easy for people to hold conflicting principles, making it impossible to create a rational (or a universal) morality. Rawls specifically mentions the American philosopher Robert Nozick's* critiques. In his "Moral Complications and Moral Structures," Nozick points out that people can come to very different conclusions about what is "self-evident" or a "necessary moral principle."⁵

But Rawls does not simply critique utilitarian or intuitionist ideas. In *A Theory of Justice* he offers an alternative way of thinking. To determine the justness of a particular system, he proposes two key principles:

- The rules that define basic freedoms should "apply to everyone equally." People should have the most liberty possible that does not interfere with other people's liberties.
- Where the system allows for inequalities, it should do so only in order to benefit each person.⁶ As an example, if someone is incentivized to carry out socially useful work that benefits other people, all individuals may agree that they are better off if that inequality exists.

While Rawls's ideas are grounded in traditional social contract theory (the liberal* idea that it is worth forgoing certain liberties if the state can guarantee security and political rights), they also offer a new and alternative approach to political theory.

1. John Rawls, *A Theory of Justice*, rev. ed. (Cambridge, MA: Belknap Press of Harvard University Press, 1999), 3.
2. See Rawls, *A Theory of Justice*, 20 cf.
3. Rawls, *A Theory of Justice*, 20 cf.
4. Rawls, *A Theory of Justice*, xviii.
5. Rawls, *A Theory of Justice*, 30.
6. Rawls, *A Theory of Justice*, 56.

MODULE 4
THE AUTHOR'S CONTRIBUTION

KEY POINTS
* Rawls's primary aim in *A Theory of Justice* is to create a new and rational way for people to build a just and fair society.
* Rawls shows how he arrives at his conclusions, allowing the reader to understand how he has formed his view of justice.
* Rawls does not require people to accept his definition of justice. He simply provides a system to help societies define what they understand by it.

Author's Aims

John Rawls's book *A Theory of Justice* is written in the tradition of liberal* political theory. Rawls proposes a theory of justice that sees the individual as a moral rational agent—capable of acting morally according to rational thought—and defends the principle of absolute freedom. His work epitomizes the idea that there can be a universal concept of human rights.* For Rawls these rights take precedence over the different ethical positions that can be found within a pluralist*society (that is, a society that permits difference, notably in political belief).

These liberal, pluralist values underlie Rawls's two key principles:
* The principle of equal freedom, according to which "each person is to have an equal right to the most extensive scheme of equal basic liberties compatible with a similar scheme of liberties for others."[1] In other words, individuals

should have freedom of action, as long as their freedom does not detract from the freedom of others.

- The principle of difference,* according to which an unequal distribution of goods in a just society can be tolerated only as far as this distribution is beneficial to the least advantaged persons of that society. Furthermore, these inequalities must be attached to offices and positions that are open to all.

Rawls acknowledges that he is indebted to the tradition of liberal thinking epitomized by the German philosopher Immanuel Kant.*2 His theories overlap with the social contract* ideas of both Kant and the Swiss-born philosopher Jean-Jacques Rousseau.*3 However, Rawls's ideas are also groundbreaking. Unlike Kant, Rawls claims that his principles of justice are not abstract, but are rooted in analysis and can be reproduced. Rawls also approaches the concept of the social contract in a new way. He uses it as a tool to help people think about the legitimacy of the way a given society is structured. In essence, Rawls claims his philosophical approach is closer to a science than an art.

> *"I have tried to present the theory of justice as a viable systematic doctrine so that the idea of maximizing the good does not hold sway by default. The criticism of teleological* theories cannot fruitfully proceed piecemeal. We must attempt to construct another kind of view which has the same virtues of clarity and system but which yields a more discriminating interpretation of our moral sensibilities."*
>
> ——John Rawls, *A Theory of Justice*

Approach

Rawls explains his goals. He discusses other ways of conceptualizing a just society and explains his objections to them. Then, carefully and methodically, he defines a number of concepts and tools—"thought experiments"*—that help the reader to follow his reasoning and test his ideas. Rawls's hypothesis is that his ideas about justice can be universally applied: they can be accepted as rational in any society at any time.

The concepts Rawls creates include: the "original position,"*[4] the "veil of ignorance,"* and "reflective equilibrium."*

According to the "original position," if a rational person had a blank canvas to create a new society, what would they want that society to achieve? How could they best create a society that meets these goals?

With the "veil of ignorance," Rawls offers us the opportunity to consider what a fair society would mean to the least advantaged member of that society. He challenges his readers to think about creating a society from a position of ignorance about their own place in that society. The veil of ignorance assumes "no one knows his place in society, his class position or social status, nor does any one know his fortune in the distribution of natural assets and abilities, his intelligence, strength, and the like."[5]

"Reflective equilibrium," finally, asks readers to reevaluate their preexisting principles by going back and forth to examine their ideas until they reach a point of equilibrium.[6]

These philosophical exercises help people define justice.

Rawls challenges the idea that history has a "given end": a supposition found in many philosophies. He also challenges the orthodoxy of liberalism and social contract theory, which says that justice is restricted by fundamental truths about human nature. Rawls argues that justice can be created through human reflection.

Contribution in Context

Rawls is not the first political theorist to discuss the concept of justice. Neither is he the first to define justice in terms of what is good for the individual within society. He built upon the thinking of writers like John Locke,* the influential English political philosopher who argued that governments rule by the consent of the governed. Locke argues that individuals do this to gain security for their natural rights: life, liberty, and property. The social contract tradition implies that a government that does not secure these natural rights is illegitimate. But Rawls goes further. He claims that people are naturally equal, and we can prove that all people should be treated as equal citizens by imagining ourselves behind the veil of ignorance in the original position.

Rawls's approach combines the social contract tradition, with the notion, following Kant, that the individual person is the primary unit that people should consider in these questions. In a theological tradition the self-centeredness of people is a weakness. For Rawls, it is an aspect of humanity that can be used to make people think *less* selfishly. By imagining they might be at the bottom of a given society, people will try to create a society that is fair to all its members.

In this combination of the selfish and the social, the practical and the moral, Rawls is a highly unique thinker. He draws upon Locke and Kant for inspiration, and Jeremy Bentham* and David Hume* for contrast, to create his own novel system for thinking rationally about justice.

---

1. John Rawls, *A Theory of Justice*, rev. ed. (Cambridge, MA: Belknap Press of Harvard University Press, 1999), 53.
2. Rawls, *A Theory of Justice*, 221–7.
3. Rawls, *A Theory of Justice*, 10.
4. Rawls, *A Theory of Justice*, 118–22.
5. Rawls, *A Theory of Justice*, 10–11.
6. Rawls, *A Theory of Justice*, 17–19.

SECTION 2
IDEAS

MODULE 5
MAIN IDEAS

KEY POINTS
- Rawls examines the theory of justice; the institutions of just societies and governments; and the ends—the desired outcomes—of a just society.
- Rawls's main argument is that people can rationally derive principles for justice by defining an acceptably fair society for the least well-off.
- Rawls aims to use a philosophical and scientific approach to the question of justice; his goal is to make his work rational and universally applicable.

Key Themes

In *A Theory of Justice* John Rawls famously defined justice as "fairness." He conceived a just society as one that had equal citizenship and equal opportunity at its heart. To explore those ideas he used an approach he called "reflective equilibrium": [1] he outlines a particular political problem or debate, examines opinions about that topic, analyzes their strengths and weaknesses, then adjusts his own ideas in light of those strengths and weaknesses. This process makes his own theory more balanced and solid. He divides his work into three parts: the theory of justice; the institutions of just societies and governments; and the ends (the desired outcomes) of a just society.

Rawls's work is motivated by his dissatisfaction with utilitarian* political theory. He argues that despite the utilitarian claim to morality this philosophy can lead to deeply amoral policy since it does not offer people a way to prioritize different virtues, or even a way to decide what virtues their society could pursue. He also points out that utilitarianism offers no mechanism by which consensus can be reached about what is most beneficial to society.

The subjectivity of intuitionism* (the process, roughly, of arriving at a solution to some philosophical problem by using intuition to weigh each side of the argument) means it cannot be used legitimately to translate ethical reasoning into social policy. Rawls outlines the weaknesses of utilitarianism and offers his own alternative: an argument that freedom must be as broad as possible, limited only when one individual's freedom of action interferes with someone else's freedoms.

> "First: each person is to have an equal right to the most extensive scheme of basic liberties compatible with a similar scheme of liberties for others.
> Second: social and economic inequalities are to be arranged so that they are both (a) reasonably expected to be to everyone's advantage, and (b) attached to positions and offices open to all."
> ——John Rawls, *A Theory of Justice*

Exploring the Ideas

Rawls starts his book by outlining the evolution of utilitarian and intuitionist ideas over the course of the period of European intellectual history known as the Enlightenment* (roughly, mid-

1600s to early 1800s) and into the Industrial Age* (the period, which began in the mid-eighteenth century, when we moved from societies founded on agriculture to societies founded on industry).

He argues that to create a fair society, people need to imagine what kind of society they would create *if they had no idea what their role in that society would be*. He calls this the "original position."* This requires an imaginary ignorance he calls "the veil of ignorance."* It is a demanding process; it is difficult to assume that one could be at the absolute bottom of society. It is as though Rawls asks his readers to wear a blindfold, clear their minds, and then orient themselves in a completely imagined society.[2]

Rawls argues that, through doing this, two key principles of a just society become self-evident: that all people must be equal citizens before the law, and that social differences and inequalities are acceptable only if they create more desirable outcomes for the whole society; to be acceptable it must also be the case that anyone could potentially hold the higher status or the better-paid jobs.[3] This is often called the "difference principle."*

Rawls compares the assumptions and outcomes of his approach with those of utilitarianism.

While Part One of Rawls's text is inherently philosophical, Part Two is distinctly political. Here, Rawls defines liberty and discusses its limitations, his ideas closely mirroring those of the philosopher John Locke.*[4] However, where Rawls innovates is in combining these ideas with ethics following the thought of Immanuel Kant.* These give his work a moral overtone: for Rawls, equating justice with fairness and personal freedom is not only the reasonable thing to do, it is the *right* thing to do. This part of the text looks at issues such as economics, the distribution of goods, and social duties. Rawls addresses issues including civil disobedience (a form of protest in which certain laws are deliberately disobeyed) and conscientious refusal (the decision not to serve in the military as a matter of conscience) which reflect the influence of events like the American civil rights movement* and the Vietnam War.*

In Part Three, Rawls offers a method for thinking about morality based on rational, agnostic, deduction rather than religious thought. Critics could, however, argue that his moral reasoning is not objective, but simply reflects Rawls's own subjective moral preferences. Rawls himself addresses the ideas of psychology* and the human desire to find meaning.[5]

Language and Expression

A Theory of Justice is a very demanding text. Rawls's audience was fellow philosophers and academics. He assumes that his readers are familiar with key political theories and already know the most important thinkers in these traditions. He moves frequently between philosophy, analogy, and discussions of historical philosophy, while introducing complicated ways to define complex concepts. This text was developed over many years and takes criticism of his earlier work into account.

Rawls's most crucial argument, his definition of "justice as fairness,"* dates back to 1958. This was the year when he first introduced the term, using it as the title of an article in *The*

Philosophical Review. Much of his work originated in papers written for academic journals and the book reflects that. It uses specialist terms, it has a complicated structure, and it makes frequent use of footnotes to offer textual evidence or further explanation. This rigorous approach gained his ideas notice and credibility within academia. Rawls's book was so thorough that even those who fundamentally disagreed with it felt compelled to explain their disagreement.

In this sense, the book can be judged to be highly influential. In fact, it has been so successful that Rawls is one of the few political theorists whose ideas are (occasionally) acknowledged by politicians and government officials.

---

1. John Rawls, *A Theory of Justice*, rev. ed. (Cambridge, MA: Belknap Press of Harvard University Press, 1999), 17–19.
2. Rawls, *A Theory of Justice*, 15–18.
3. Rawls, *A Theory of Justice*, 52–64.
4. See John Locke, *Locke on Toleration*, ed. Richard Vernon (Cambridge: Cambridge University Press, 2010), for his views on how much toleration and freedom are proper in society.
5. Rawls, *A Theory of Justice*, 429–33.

MODULE 6
SECONDARY IDEAS

KEY POINTS

- Key amongst the secondary ideas in Rawls's work is the concept of the "original position": * the blank canvas upon which a just society can be created.
- Several scholars have studied Rawls's tools and concepts, believing them to be valuable in their own right.
- While Part Three of *A Theory of Justice* has been overlooked, there is growing academic interest in this section of Rawls's work.

Other Ideas

One of the most important secondary ideas in John Rawls's *A Theory of Justice* is the thought experiment* he calls the "original position"—an imaginative exercise he uses to draw conclusions about the nature of justice and its relationship to the state. Rawls uses a number of techniques to help his reader step outside his or her awareness of their own societal position, allowing them to consider how true justice would look to people no matter what position they occupy within society. He calls this lack of awareness of status (of wealth, profession, abilities, intellect, or even individual moral preferences) the "veil of ignorance,"* arguing that thinkers adopting the original position can achieve consensus on the nature of justice. This is because the original position "excludes the knowledge of those contingencies which set men at odds and allow them to be guided by their prejudices."[1]

Another key idea in the text is the concept of "reflective equilibrium":* going back to ideas, reflecting on their strengths and weaknesses, and adjusting these ideas to take account of those strengths and weaknesses. Although this concept is not discussed at great length in the text, its influence pervades every argument Rawls makes. While *A Theory of Justice* is a long and in some ways repetitive book, the repetition occurs as a result of Rawls refining his ideas in order to reach a point of reflective equilibrium (achieved at roughly 500 pages of discussion).

It is difficult to speak of Rawls's secondary ideas in isolation. They are closely interwoven and Rawls uses them as tools to show the readers how his thought has developed. In other words, his secondary ideas give shape to the content of his thought on justice and fairness.

> "We may define self-respect (or self-esteem) as having two aspects. First of all, as we noted earlier, it includes a person's sense of his own value, his secure conviction that his conception of his good, his plan of life, is worth carrying out. And second, self-respect implies a confidence in one's ability, so far as it is within one's power, to fulfill one's intentions."
>
> ——John Rawls, *A Theory of Justice*

Exploring the Ideas

Rawls believes that his concept of the original position is vital for helping people come to rational, universal conclusions about social justice. He emphasizes that the original position is a hypothetical construct. It is an idea, however, that has been criticized for being impossible to imagine. Rawls replies that "the hypothetical nature of the original position invites the question: why should we take any interest in it, moral or otherwise? Recall the answer: the conditions embodied in the description of this situation are ones that we do in fact accept. Or if we do not, then we can be persuaded to do so by philosophical considerations of the sort occasionally introduced."[2]

This statement is remarkably confident. Rawls has thought about justice for many years. His approach is careful and methodical. As a result, he makes the (very large) assumption that other people who reflect on these issues equally carefully will draw the same conclusions.

Why bother, then, with the thought experiment of the original position? Because we already accept its premises, and even if we do not, Rawls can convince us that they are correct.

In this sense, Rawls's theory runs the danger of becoming an ideology proper: a view of the world that is certain of its assumptions and assertive in its prescriptions.

Overlooked

Part Three of *A Theory of Justice* is one of the most neglected sections of Rawls's text.[3] Rawls discusses justice in relation to moral psychology* and introduces the idea of a "sentiment of justice"—the idea that the individuals who make up a given society share a common view of justice. Following this discussion, Rawls looks at the outcome for a society that shares a common understanding of justice. He argues that when a society's ideas about justice align with their social values, the society can be called well ordered. A well-ordered society is likely to enjoy stability. Rawls also claims that when a people share a common sentiment of justice, it helps society remain committed to justice as a common good.

It is only recently that scholars have shown revived interest in this part of Rawls's theory. One relevant example is the work of the American philosopher Paul Weithman.*[4] His work addresses Rawls's shift from his original theory of justice to subsequent work in which he discusses political liberalism.*[5] Weithman argues that *A Theory of Justice* is not as individualist and Kantian—founded on the ideas of Immanuel Kant*—as many other scholars have believed. He uses Rawls's ideas about stability and the sentiment of justice to suggest that Rawls's philosophy relies on a "sense of justice."[6] This refers to people's capacity to develop a shared morality upon which the stability of a well-ordered society is based.

---

1. John Rawls, *A Theory of Justice*, rev. ed. (Cambridge, MA: Belknap Press of Harvard University Press, 1999), 15–17.
2. Rawls, *Theory of Justice*, 514.
3. Rawls, *Theory of Justice*, 347–514.
4. Paul J. Weithman, *Why Political Liberalism? On John Rawls's Political Turn* (New York and Oxford: Oxford University Press, 2011).
5. Particularly in the collected essays in John Rawls, *Political Liberalism* (New York: Columbia University Press, 1993).
6. According to Rawls, "A sense of justice is an effective desire to apply and act from the principles of justice and so from the point of view of justice." Rawls, *A Theory of Justice*, 497.

MODULE 7
ACHIEVEMENT

KEY POINTS

* Rawls wanted to convince others that his approach to justice was reasonable, rational, and achievable (at least in theory).
* The painstaking explanation of his ideas, his tools for thinking about the ideal society, and the quality of his philosophical arguments all demanded serious attention.
* While Rawls influenced the debate on justice and became one of the most important thinkers in this area, he was limited by his reliance on the liberal* tradition and its universalist assumptions (that is, its assumptions that its arguments are applicable in all circumstances).

Assessing the Argument

In *A Theory of Justice* John Rawls assumes that his theory is applicable within well-ordered societies—but it may be that not all societies in the world reflect Rawls's criteria of "well ordered."[1]

One example would be a society that is hierarchical and characterized by an overarching ethical conception that informs its structure (as an example, a monarchy in which there are social inequalities that do not arise from the merits and capabilities of its citizens). Yet this society could still guarantee a decent level of basic rights to its members.[2] Rawls discusses this possibility in his later book *The Law of Peoples*. He uses an imaginary example: the state of Kazanistan. Rawls argues that liberals should not intervene in the affairs of this society, since this would be in breach of the liberal principle of tolerance. This example represents a limitation to the ideas that Rawls's theories have universal validity.

Scholars such as the American political theorist Charles Beitz* and the German philosopher Thomas Pogge* have argued (in different ways) that Rawls's theory regarding equal liberty and the principle of difference* can be applied universally; in contrast to Rawls himself, Beitz and Pogge argue that the cultural differences between nations do not necessarily represent a limitation on the possibility of recognizing universal human rights,* such as social and economic rights, and global social justice. In *The Law of Peoples*, Rawls argues that only fundamental human rights are universal.

> "Without denying that actual political achievement of the ideal is important, he [Rawls] believed that a well-grounded belief in its achievability can reconcile us to the world. So long as we are justifiably confident that a self-sustaining and just collective life among human beings is realistically possible, we may hope that we or others will someday, somewhere, achieve it—and can then also work towards this achievement ... political philosophy can provide an inspiration that can banish the dangers of resignation and cynicism and can enhance the value of our lives even today."
> ——Thomas Pogge, *John Rawls: His Life and Theory of Justice*

Achievement in Context

Even those who disagree with Rawls praise his work. One of his sharpest critics, the Canadian-born Marxist philosopher Gerald Cohen,* writes that "at most two books in the history of Western political philosophy* have a claim to be regarded as greater than *A Theory of Justice*: Plato's* *Republic* and Hobbes's* *Leviathan*."³ As soon as *A Theory of Justice* was published it was considered an essential text. Rawls's ideas pulled the focus of political theory away from the utilitarian* notion of the "common good" and toward the good of the individual.

Rawls was writing in the midst of the Cold War*—a long period of military and diplomatic tensions characterized, in part, by its competing ideologies of democracy (the "Western Bloc" of the United States and its allies) and communism (the "Eastern Bloc" of the Soviet Union* and the nations aligned to it). He sought to free political theory from its reliance on utilitarian moral philosophy and intuitionist* method (according to which intuition is a useful tool in the process of solving philosophical problems by weighing alternative solutions).

Instead, his aim was to create a liberal, contractarian* understanding of justice: an understanding, based on liberty and the idea that we agree on the condition of social life by contractually agreeing to certain obligations, that could be universally agreed on and achieved.⁴

While he succeeded in his desire to move political theory away from utilitarianism, the hope that his ideas offered a universal blueprint for creating justice, however, has not been thoroughly tested by subsequent developments in global politics. Universality is not always the aim of a political theory, nor does every society wish to achieve a universally applicable model of government. The Cold War may have obscured that fact. The Soviet Union and the

United States both sought to convince the world that their system was the best way to order society. Both nations believed they should give the gift of their civilizations to the world. Although Rawls rejects the belief in a predefined end of history that Marxism and liberalism can both display, he nonetheless reverts to similar universalist tendencies. Having spent two decades thinking about justice, Rawls asserts that his conclusions are those that any rational person would come to.

Despite this limitation, *A Theory of Justice* arguably became the most influential work of political theory of the late twentieth century. It continues to be influential, indeed central, in the work of prominent thinkers like the Nobel Prize-winning philosopher and economist Amartya Sen.*[5]

Limitations

Rawls reflected on the controversial issue of whether or not his work applied universally in his later work. In his book *The Law of Peoples*,[6] he presents his thinking on international justice. Other scholars have also debated whether his theory can be globally applied and whether it works for societies that are not traditionally liberal.[7]

In *A Theory of Justice* Rawls discusses applying his ideas on an international scale. He claims that his thought experiment* of the "original position"* would only justify the first principle of justice: the right of each nation to be equally free. In this sense, Rawls's theory is universal. It justifies the ideas that nations should be equally free to exercise self-determination and self-defense.[8]

Rawls said that his second principle of justice—about

distribution of opportunity—does not apply universally since it is based on a community that shares a common sense of justice. Even regions like the European Union, a body supposedly based on shared European values and identity, have faced considerable challenges in this area. It is hard to create a just system of apportioning funding and deciding on appropriate government spending policies. This limits, and perhaps even refutes, Rawls's theory of universal principles of justice.

It is, perhaps, the case that these principles apply only within the domestic context of a liberal society—one in which all members share a similar sense of justice.[9]

---

1. For an introductory discussion of the concept of "well-ordered society," see Thomas Pogge and Michelle Kosch, *John Rawls: His Life and Theory of Justice* (Oxford and New York: Oxford University Press, 2007), 137–9.
2. See John Rawls, *The Law of Peoples: With "The Idea of Public Reason Revisited"* (Cambridge, MA: Harvard University Press, 1999).
3. G. A. Cohen, *Rescuing Justice and Equality* (Cambridge, MA: Harvard University Press, 2008), 11.
4. John Rawls, *A Theory of Justice*, rev. ed. (Cambridge, MA: Belknap Press of Harvard University Press, 1999), 10.
5. See Amartya Sen, *The Idea of Justice* (Cambridge, MA: Belknap Press of Harvard University Press, 2009).
6. Rawls, *Law of Peoples*.
7. Thomas Nagel, "The Problem of Global Justice," *Philosophy & Public Affairs* 33, no. 2 (2005): 113–47; Thomas Pogge, *World Poverty and Human Rights: Cosmopolitan Responsibilities and Reforms*, 2nd ed. (Cambridge: Polity, 2008); Charles R. Beitz, *Political Theory and International Relations*, 2nd ed. (Princeton, N. J.: Princeton University Press, 1999); Alasdair MacIntyre, *Whose Justice? Which Rationality?* (London: Duckworth, 1988).
8. Rawls, *A Theory of Justice*, 331–2.
9. Rawls, *A Theory of Justice*, 497.

MODULE 8
PLACE IN THE AUTHOR'S WORK

KEY POINTS
- *A Theory of Justice* is the distillation of Rawls's work as an academic.
- In the book Rawls develops his earlier ideas about social justice, going beyond simple exploration of a concept to develop an entire system for understanding justice.
- *A Theory of Justice* made Rawls's name famous within the field of political philosophy;* he spent the rest of his career refining his arguments and responding to his many admirers and critics.

Positioning

By the time John Rawls published *A Theory of Justice* in 1971, he had already studied and worked at some of the world's most elite universities, including Oxford and Harvard. This was, however, his first publication in book form and it became the most relevant and acclaimed text he published. Parts of the work are derived from Rawls's previous papers and academic articles. He began work on the book itself in 1962. After several revisions, it was eventually published in 1971. By then Rawls was 50 years old and the chairman of the philosophy department at Harvard.

A Theory of Justice is a compilation and expansion of Rawls's earlier work. The issue of justice is central in nearly all of his texts. Rawls's biographer, the German-born philosopher Thomas Pogge,* notes that Rawls's lifelong study of justice was initially derived from his Christian religious ethos. It then became even more potent after he left his faith. Rawls needed to find a suitable alternative to religion on which to ground his social ethics.[1] The third section of the book can be seen as a reflection of Rawls's own social involvement. Outside academia he was a member of various social justice movements and opposed the Vietnam War.*

In 1999 Rawls published a second edition of *A Theory of Justice*. Although he did not abandon or even significantly change any of his main ideas or philosophical arguments in this edition, in the preface he acknowledges a number of criticisms that he deemed especially important or valid. He then directs the reader's attention to his subsequent revisions. Rawls can be seen as a scholar who was seeking to refine—rather than to reinvent or discard—his earlier ideas. Even his revisions are in keeping with his belief in "reflective equilibrium":* nearly all of them are to do with making his definitions and ideas clearer and more precise.[2]

> *"Despite many criticisms of the original work, I still accept its main outlines and defend its central doctrines. Of course, I wish, as one might expect, that I had done certain things differently, and I would now make a number of important revisions. But if I were writing A Theory of Justice over again, I would not write, as authors sometimes say, a completely different book."*
>
> —— John Rawls, preface to the revised edition,
> *A Theory of Justice*

Integration

Rawls's body of work is extremely coherent. His entire body of work can be viewed as a discussion of a few key themes: social justice, fairness, human rights,* social ethics. These themes are discussed repeatedly, as Rawls engages in a process of making them more philosophically coherent, more politically relevant, and, he hoped, more persuasive.

We may consider *A Theory of Justice* to fundamentally describe Rawls's thought. In his subsequent publications, he is engaged in two main tasks. The first is that of clarifying, restating, or revising aspects of his theory by responding to his critics (his second book publication, the collection of essays entitled *Political Liberalism*,[3] was dedicated to this, as was the revised edition of *A Theory of Justice* published in 1999).

The second of Rawls's tasks was to develop and expand certain aspects of his theory. While *A Theory of Justice* is concerned mainly with domestic justice, Rawls's final publication, *The Law of Peoples*,[4] discusses justice in political theory with reference to the international political context. Here Rawls elaborates on the theory of international justice, which is briefly sketched in *A Theory of Justice*.[5] He developed these ideas further in a public lecture given for the human rights organization Amnesty International.*[6] Rawls sought to assess how far his ideas can be applied to the problems of international relations.

Significance

Rawls's boy of literary work is compact, consistent, and strictly focused on the subject of his academic research: studying the theory of a just society. In methodological and conceptual terms, Rawls's academic production remains consistent, even if subject to revisions and changes. The highly specialized vocabulary that Rawls defines in *A Theory of Justice* was to inform the entire political-theory debate in subsequent decades and remained substantially unaltered across various publications.

Although *A Theory of Justice* has provoked a number of critiques and refutations, its influence is unquestionable. Rawls shaped the scholarly debate about political theory and his intellectual and academic achievements could scarcely have been of higher quality or greater import.

Rawls's work was so influential that he was awarded the National Humanities Medal by President Bill Clinton* in 1999— a medal awarded for work that deepens the nation's understanding of the humanities. During a brief speech explaining the reasons John Rawls was being honored, President Clinton noted the impact his work had on him and his political development, as well as on his wife, Hillary. Clinton said that "when Hillary and I were in law school, we were among the millions" moved by Rawls's book. Rawls, Clinton said, "helped a whole generation of learned Americans revive their faith in democracy itself."[7]

---

1. See John Rawls, "50 Years After Hiroshima," *Dissent* (summer 1995): 323–7. Also, Thomas Pogge and Michelle Kosch, *John Rawls: His Life and Theory of Justice* (Oxford and New York: Oxford University Press, 2007), 18–19.

2. John Rawls, *A Theory of Justice*, rev. ed. (Cambridge, MA: Belknap Press of Harvard University Press, 1999), xi–xvi.
3. John Rawls, *Political Liberalism* (New York: Columbia University Press, 1993).
4. John Rawls, *The Law of Peoples: With "The Idea of Public Reason Revisited"* (Cambridge, MA: Harvard University Press, 1999).
5. Rawls refers to the idea of the law of nations, which subsequently became the law of peoples, in paragraph 58 of *A Theory of Justice*, 331–5.
6. The lecture was then published as a paper in John Rawls, *Collected Papers*, ed. Samuel Richard Freeman (Cambridge, MA: Harvard University Press, 1999).
7. William J. Clinton, in *Public Papers of Presidents of the United States: William J. Clinton* (1999), 1628–9.

SECTION 3
IMPACT

MODULE 9
THE FIRST RESPONSES

KEY POINTS

* Rawls is criticized by a number of thinkers on both the left and right of the political spectrum, especially on the issue of equality.
* Rawls admits that the issue of equality is the weakest link in his chain of reasoning.
* The ideas expressed in *A Theory of Justice* are so compelling that they sharpen the arguments of everyone involved in the debate, including thinkers who criticize Rawls's assumptions or goals.

Criticism

Only a few years after the publication of John Rawls's *A Theory of Justice* in 1971, the American philosopher Robert Nozick* published work arguing against Rawls's ideas of making society more equal through taxation and redistribution.¹ More criticism emerged from communitarian* thinkers. Communitarians reject the idea that humans can develop moral concepts independently of the society and community to which they belong.

Communitarian thinkers such as the Scottish philosopher Alasdair MacIntyre* and the Canadian philosopher Charles Taylor* were critical of the substance of Rawls's theory. They criticize the idea that humans were capable of moral impartiality and argue that the way Rawls prioritizes "the right" over "the good" is problematic.² MacIntyre argues that an individual's ethical ideas cannot be understood as disembodied from the cultural and historical tradition to which they belong—meaning that the idea that there is a universal, human agreement on what is "right" is ahistorical and misleading.³ Similarly, Taylor says it is impossible to abstract moral principles from the "social matrix" in which they are developed; in other words, what is right for a society cannot be separated from what is good for a person.⁴ Another communitarian critic of Rawls, the American philosopher Michael Sandel,* challenges Rawls's idea of the original position.*⁵ Sandel argues that it is impossible for an individual to be capable of abstract moral reason outside a given social and moral context.

Scholars on the left also criticize Rawls. The Marxist scholar Gerald Cohen* argues that Rawls's version of equality is not egalitarian enough. According to Cohen, a truly egalitarian theory of justice cannot justify the degree of inequality that the Rawlsian principle of difference* concedes. He rejects Rawls's idea that inequality should be tolerated if it can be seen to benefit the least advantaged members of a society.⁶

> "One of the most serious weaknesses was in the account of liberty, the defects of which were pointed out by H. L. A. Hart in his critical discussion of 1973 ... A second serious weakness of the original edition was its account of primary goods ... The revisions are too many to note here, but they do not, I think, depart in any important way from the view of the original edition."
>
> —— John Rawls, preface to the revised edition, *A Theory of Justice*

Responses

Rawls addressed his critics in a number of different lectures and publications, and in a revised edition of *A Theory of Justice* (1999). His response to criticism was to incorporate any criticism that could weaken his theory into his argument, reflect on it, and adjust his ideas where he felt the criticism was valid. He also proposed counterarguments to his critics, which stimulated further academic debate.

In the revised edition of *A Theory of Justice*, Rawls addresses early criticism of his ideas from the British philosopher H. L. A. Hart.* Hart pointed out problems with Rawls's concept of liberty.[7] In response Rawls proposes revisions to his account of liberty. In others papers and lectures, Rawls answers his communitarian critics.[8] In his collection of essays *Political Liberalism*, Rawls points out that his theory is in fact a theory of *political* liberalism.* This means that he is discussing ethics in the context of the political sphere. This does not interfere with other ethical conceptions, as long as these are reasonable and do not violate the principles of justice. Political liberalism is not an overarching moral conception (unlike a religion); instead, it takes into account pluralism*—a political system that can accommodate people from a number of different backgrounds, notably in terms of ethnicity or religion.

Having clarified these points, Rawls adheres to the substance of his theory; he does not alter his ideas about justice within societies.

Conflict and Consensus

As we have seen, much important criticism came from communitarian thinkers. Particularly influential were arguments made by the philosophers Michael Sandel and Charles Taylor that individuals have comprehensive conceptions of the good and that these concepts inform our idea of justice and what is right. This counters Rawls's idea that what is *right* would, in a just society, take precedence over what is *good*.

Perhaps the most important development in Rawls's theory came with the publication of his book *The Law of Peoples*. This uses his fundamental theory of justice as a basis to discuss the issue of justice on an international scale.[9] In this book Rawls develops and significantly modifies the idea about international justice that he had briefly presented in *A Theory of Justice*. These modifications cannot, however, be primarily accredited to criticism from other scholars. They were due to Rawls's own awareness of the limits of his theory in the international political context.

The general perception amongst scholars is that no critique of Rawls's theory dealt a fatal blow to his work. Rawls's theory remains among the most accomplished examples of scholarship in the field of political theory. Critics of Rawls are still active, and indeed still critical—but his work remains a key reference in contemporary political theory, provoking original thought and debate.

1. See, for example, Robert Nozick, *Anarchy, State, and Utopia* (Oxford: Blackwell, 1974). On the basis of the same theory, other political conceptions, such as the minimal state and anarchism, have been defended as ways of minimizing interference in people's negative freedom.
2. See Alasdair C. MacIntyre, *After Virtue: A Study in Moral Theory*, 3rd ed. (Notre Dame, IN: University of Notre Dame Press, 2007); and Charles Taylor, *Human Agency and Language: Philosophical Papers 1* (Cambridge: Cambridge University Press, 1985).
3. MacIntyre, *After Virtue*.
4. Taylor, *Human Agency and Language*.
5. Michael J. Sandel, *Liberalism and the Limits of Justice*, 2nd ed. (Cambridge: Cambridge University Press, 1998).
6. G. A. Cohen, *Rescuing Justice and Equality* (Cambridge, MA: Harvard University Press, 2008).
7. H. L. A. Hart, "Rawls on Liberty and Its Priority," *University of Chicago Law Review* 40, no. 3 (1973): 534–55.
8. John Rawls, *Political Liberalism* (New York: Columbia University Press, 1993).
9. John Rawls, *The Law of Peoples: With "The Idea of Public Reason Revisited"* (Cambridge, MA: Harvard University Press, 1999).

MODULE 10
THE EVOLVING DEBATE

KEY POINTS
- Supporters of Rawls have extended his thought into the sphere of international relations and global justice.
- Scholars sometimes self-identify as "Rawlsian" in order to express their general agreement with Rawls's ideas.
- *A Theory of Justice* continues to influence current political debates; Rawlsian ideas have been used, for example, to discuss economic and environmental issues.

Uses and Problems

Rawls's *A Theory of Justice* is still used to discuss current political and social issues. Scholars have asked what Rawls has to say with regard to global justice in an increasingly interconnected world. How does justice as fairness* relate to global environmental concerns? Which circumstances and reasons might determine a just war? Which moral issues are raised by the use of new military technologies, such as drones?

Rawls's work provides a robust analytical framework to reflect on possible answers to these questions. Many of the issues have been tackled in the scholarly literature that has emerged in response to *A Theory of Justice*.

Rawls's conception of fundamental rights has been criticized as minimalist. His work is primarily concerned with political and civil rights, and does not address redistributive principles such as social and economic rights. This omission provokes reactions from those scholars who think that inequality on a global scale is an injustice that political institutions have a moral obligation to address. The philosopher Thomas Pogge,* for example, has developed the idea of global redistributive tax*[1] and the empowerment of international institutions. The political theorist Charles Beitz*[2] has argued for the need to fully incorporate economic and social rights into universal human rights.* These ideas conflict with Rawls's minimalist theories of human rights. Rawls does not prescribe specific actions or institutions for promoting human rights. He simply advances a means for thinking about these issues rationally with the assumption that it is rational to believe that thinking about these issues will lead to them being advanced.

> "John Rawls's The Law of Peoples represents a culmination of his reflections on how we might reasonably and peacefully live together in a just world. My aim in this article is partly to pay homage by being more royalist than the king: I argue that Rawls's theory of justice can and should be extended ... The result is a conception of global justice that is more liberal in Rawls's own terms."
> ——Andrew Kuper, "Rawlsian Global Justice: Beyond the Law of Peoples to a Cosmopolitan Law of Persons"

Schools of Thought

Rawls's work resulted in a school of thought referred to as "Rawlsian thought" or "Rawlsianism." In his biography of Rawls,

Thomas Pogge provides a list of Rawls's most influential students. Many of them are among the most influential contemporary political thinkers;[3] it should be noted, however, that they often adjust, correct, or reinterpret important components of Rawls's theory to suit their own interests and arguments.

When *A Theory of Justice* was first published, globalization*—the convergence of global economies and cultures—and the interconnectedness of human existence were not as relevant as they became in the decades that followed. This is why the international dimension of *A Theory of Justice* is rather minimal. Rawlsian thinkers have built upon Rawls's theory, applying it to the global social and political spheres. Thinkers such as Beitz and Pogge disagree with Rawls's minimalism in global justice. Their cosmopolitan* theories—belonging to a branch of liberal* political theory characterized by a commitment to the idea of a universal form of citizenship—seek recognition for universal human rights in the civil, political, economic, and social spheres.

Rawls proposed a narrower conception of international justice; in his work, freedom is conceived as having universal appeal and equality is closely related to domestic politics. Thinkers such as Pogge, however, have advocated extending Rawls's principles of justice to the universal sphere, which has led to a theory of global redistributive justice.[4]

Rawls's work radically changed debate in the field of political theory. But while his theory is highly influential and has shaped the thinking of many scholars, the field of political theory has become somewhat fixated with Rawls's work; this perhaps might undermine its capacity to contribute to innovation.[5]

In Current Scholarship

Among scholars who identify Rawls as a primary influence on their thought are Charles Beitz, Thomas Pogge, the American philosophers Thomas Nagel,* Thomas Scanlon,* Joshua Cohen, Samuel Freeman,* and Paul Weithman,* and the Irish philosopher Onora O'Neill.* Cosmopolitan thinkers such as Beitz, the American philosopher Martha Nussbaum, and the British political theorist Simon Caney use his ideas to speak about issues of global justice. Much of this debate centers on whether Rawls's view of international justice, largely developed in his book *The Law of Peoples*, guarantees sufficient standards of justice. Another important scholar who has contributed to this debate is the influential Indian-born philosopher Amartya Sen,* who discusses the problem of inequality and how poverty can be measured.[6]

Although the issues of global justice and inequality have been addressed widely in the political debate, others, such as the issue of environmental preservation and the idea of intergenerational justice, are still emerging. The British philosopher Brian Barry* has discussed the limitations of Rawls's theory from the point of view of intergenerational issues—but this is a debate that will continue to be updated. Demands for justice will keep arising in new domestic and international political contexts.[7]

Similarly, although the question of a just war is centuries old, the "new wars" fought since 2000 pose new questions on the morality of war and its regulation; while Rawls does not address these questions directly, answers may be found through use of the conceptual framework that his theory provides.

---

1. Thomas W. Pogge, "Eradicating Systemic Poverty: Brief for a Global Resources Dividend," *Journal of Human Development* 2, no. 1 (2001): 59–77.
2. Charles R. Beitz, *Political Theory and International Relations*, 2nd ed. (Princeton: Princeton University Press, 1999).
3. Thomas Winfried Pogge and Michelle Kosch, *John Rawls: His Life and Theory of Justice* (London: Oxford University Press, 2007), 24.
4. For a version of this proposal see Pogge, "Eradicating Systemic Poverty."
5. Consider, for example, the criticism raised by Berkowitz in this respect. Peter Berkowitz, "The Ambiguities of Rawls's Influence," *Perspectives on Politics* 4, no.1 (2006): 121–33.
6. Amartya Sen, *Inequality Reexamined* (Oxford: Clarendon Press, 1992) and *Development as Freedom* (Oxford: Oxford University Press, 2001).
7. Brian Barry, *Theories of Justice* (Hemel Hempstead: Harvester Wheatsheaf, 1989).

MODULE 11
IMPACT AND INFLUENCE TODAY

KEY POINTS

- Although more than 40 years have passed since the publication of *A Theory of Justice*, it is cited in more publications in more fields of thought than ever before.
- A number of scholars remain unconvinced by Rawls's discussion of equality; they have sought to build their own innovative solutions to problems of equality.
- Even Rawls's harshest critics continue to cite his work as a theory that must be reckoned with.

Position

John Rawls's seminal work *A Theory of Justice* is perhaps more relevant now than it was when it was written.

In 2010 the leading political theorist Amartya Sen* published his acclaimed work *The Idea of Justice*[1]—a significant portion of which is dedicated to a discussion of Rawls's theory. Sen was a colleague of Rawls at Harvard. Their exchange of ideas went on for decades, producing some of the most important contributions to political theory in the contemporary scholarly debate. In *The Idea of Justice*, Sen proposes a thorough and innovative critique of Rawls's theory of justice. His main criticism of Rawls's thesis is that it defines justice in terms of perfect principles upon which a just society should rely. According to Sen, this "transcendental institutionalism" (that is, the assumptions it makes about the nature and role of the institution) should be abandoned; in its place there should be assessment and comparison of existing institutions and their social impact. He claims that thinkers such as Jeremy Bentham,* Adam Smith,* and Karl Marx were already engaged in this process of comparison. Sen calls this "realization-focused comparison" and places himself in this tradition.

This rather pragmatic approach to the scholarly debate comes from Sen's underlying assumption that reasoning does not deliver the universal and incontrovertible principles that liberal* thinkers expect. This does not happen even under the conditions of the Rawlsian thought experiment* of the "original position."* Furthermore, even if reason did have the capacity to determine perfect principles of justice, human beings would not necessarily follow its dictates. Sen argues that injustice would therefore still take place. By proposing an alternative way to develop a theory of justice, Sen offers another contribution to the debate on Rawls. This may spark further reaction and continue to perpetuate the debate about justice in the field of political theory.

> "The development of Western democracies in the twentieth century has placed increasingly severe strains on liberal concepts of social justice. Two major factors involved in this process are international competition with non-capitalist* societies, and continual internal conflict between elites and the dispossessed ... Given these developments, it is not surprising that a book such as John Rawls's A Theory of Justice might touch off considerable controversy—perhaps more than any other work in social theory since Keynes' General Theory."
> —— Barry Clark and Herbert Gintis, "Rawlsian Justice and Economic Systems"

Interaction

Surprisingly, Rawls's work is not primarily challenged by the people he himself openly disagreed with—the utilitarians* and intuitionists.* This may be because his book was so influential that these schools of thought fell out of fashion. But groups exist, on both sides of the political spectrum, that do not agree with Rawls's text.

One of Rawls's more famous critics is the American philosopher Robert Nozick.* Nozick's work *Anarchy, State, and Utopia*, published in 1974, is highly critical of Rawls. Nozick criticizes Rawls's ideas about social justice, especially the idea of redistribution. Nozick is a libertarian.* The main concern of libertarianism is the right of individuals to act autonomously and to avoid as many obligations and entanglements to society as possible. Nozick is against the idea of encouraging social equality through collecting taxes and distributing benefits. What for Rawls is social justice and in keeping with the difference principle,* for Nozick amounts to nothing but state-sanctioned theft.[2]

Coming from the opposite direction are Marxist thinkers like the philosopher Gerald Cohen.* Like Nozick, Cohen is critical of Rawls's discussion of equality, but for the opposite reason. Cohen argues that the justice Rawls describes actually requires total equality. As a result Rawls's difference principle—which allows for different amounts of wealth and status if these inequalities benefit society—is actually a way of watering down his whole theory of justice.[3]

The Continuing Debate

Much of the debate that surrounds Rawls's work is concerned with whether the way he applies his ideas goes far enough, or how it can be applied in new ways or to new circumstances. Unsurprisingly, the focus of political theories changes as political issues change. This explains, at least in part, why Rawlsian ideas are now being debated in fields like economics and environmentalism.

Economic thinkers like Amartya Sen and the American scholar Nien-hê Hsieh* use Rawls's principles of justice to think about what is required to create a just economic order. Hsieh draws on *A Theory of Justice* and on Rawls's later book *The Law of Peoples* to apply Rawlsian ideas to the issue of business ethics. He uses Rawlsian ideas to argue that transnational corporations—corporations that operate across international borders—have an obligation to assist people in developing economies. He suggests they should implement just policies such as labor rights and environmental protections.[4]

Recent environmental writing, like that of the Norwegian political theorist Oluf Langhelle,* applies Rawls's ideas to include environmental goods. This is similar to the way Rawls discusses economic goods and wealth in *A Theory of Justice*.[5] In doing this, Langhelle is following in the tradition of Charles Beitz,* who applied Rawlsian ideas to the issue of global social justice.

1. Amartya Sen, *The Idea of Justice* (Cambridge, MA: Belknap Press of Harvard University Press, 2009).
2. Robert Nozick, "Distributive Justice," *Philosophy & Public Affairs* (1973): 79–81.
3. The most relevant critical observation on Rawls can be found in G. A. Cohen, *Rescuing Justice and Equality* (Cambridge, MA: Harvard University Press, 2008).
4. Nien-hê Hsieh, "The Obligations of Transnational Corporations: Rawlsian Justice and the Duty of Assistance," *Business Ethics Quarterly* 14, no. 4 (2004): 643.
5. Oluf Langhelle, "Sustainable Development and Social Justice: Expanding the Rawlsian Framework of Global Justice," *Environmental Values* 9, no. 3 (2000): 295–323.

MODULE 12
WHERE NEXT?

KEY POINTS

- Rawls's *A Theory of Justice*, its related principles of fairness and limited equality, and its many analytical tools made it an instant classic.

- Interest in Rawls's work continues to be extremely high. Many political thinkers believe his text must be acknowledged in any discussion that touches upon its key themes.

- Thinkers interested in a wide array of issues now use Rawls's ideas about justice. These issues range from development* and human rights* to the environment.

Potential

The influence of John Rawls's seminal text *A Theory of Justice* has been enormous in its own field and in related academic contexts. More than 40 years after the book was published, political theorists call it one of the most significant (if not the most important) contributions to the field. Perhaps the clearest indication of Rawls's stature was accorded to him by one of his sharpest critics, the philosopher Gerald Cohen.*[1] Cohen commented that "at most two books in the history of Western political philosophy* have a claim to be regarded as greater than *A Theory of Justice*: Plato's* *Republic* and Hobbes's* *Leviathan*."[2] The works of the Ancient Greek philosopher Plato and the English philosopher Thomas Hobbes are not simply regarded as classics. They are seen as indispensable texts for understanding political societies and philosophy. For a critic to place Rawls in the company of great thinkers like these speaks volumes for Rawls's reputation as an original and challenging thinker.

The fields of moral philosophy, epistemology (the study of knowledge), and economics have also been significantly influenced by Rawls's theory. This is not surprising, as his ideas delve deeply into questions of morals. How should people and societies make judgments about what is morally right? However, Rawls himself stated that his theory only applies to the most fundamental structure of society.[3] This makes it hard to estimate the impact of *A Theory of Justice* in contexts outside political theory and its related fields.

> *"My hope is that justice as fairness* will seem reasonable and useful, even if not fully convincing, to a wide range of thoughtful political opinions and thereby express an essential part of the common core of the democratic tradition."*
>
> —— John Rawls, preface to the revised edition, *A Theory of Justice*

Future Directions

The complexity of Rawls's theory means that his ideas continue to be reinterpreted and applied to new fields of study. Today, the Rawlsian school of thought is among the most influential of political theories. Even thinkers who have criticized Rawls engage with his ideas and with the way his ideas have been developed by Rawlsian thinkers.

Rawls's approach to justice continues to shape the way other thinkers deal with this concept and how it should govern society. Scholars from other disciplines also borrow from his work. Academics interested in sustainable development, for example, use the Rawlsian argument that acting in a sustainable way is the right—that is moral or fair—thing to do, both for people today and for future generations.

But not all of Rawls's ideas work perfectly in practice. Scholars of international politics have not yet found a way to reconcile the ideas held by different nation states about what is just or good. Nonetheless, Rawls's work resonates with the need to create universally acceptable norms within international affairs. The more human beings live, trade, work, and engage politically at a global level, the greater the need for a common understanding of what is meant by justice.

Summary

A Theory of Justice inspired and continues to inspire scholars from a number of fields interested in the idea of social justice. Philosophers, lawmakers, war protestors, human rights activists, and numerous other professionals have been inspired and challenged by Rawls. His original and highly open approach focuses on creating a society that best cares for all of its citizens. In contrast with many other political philosophers, Rawls shows his readers how to replicate his thinking. This allows them to imagine for themselves what institutions and practices are most likely to achieve a state that they would be willing to live in—even if they were at the bottom of the social ladder.

Although written in 1971, Rawls's thought experiments* and the concepts he derives from them are perhaps more useful now than ever. Issues such as globalization,* environmental degradation, the changing nature of employment, and the power of multinational corporations all need people to think about justice, equality, and fairness. As Rawls argues:"Justice is the first virtue of social institutions, as truth is of systems of thought."[4]

A Theory of Justice will remain a work that provides challenging ideas, philosophical reflection, and political and social inspiration to its readers.

---

1. G. A. Cohen, *Rescuing Justice and Equality* (Cambridge, MA: Harvard University Press, 2008).
2. Cohen, *Rescuing Justice*, 11.
3. Louis-Philippe Hodgson, "Why the Basic Structure?" *Canadian Journal of Philosophy* 42, no. 3–4 (2012): 303–34.
4. Rawls, *A Theory of Justice*, 3.

GLOSSARY OF TERMS

1. **Amnesty International:** an international organization founded to support human rights (notably those of people imprisoned for their political beliefs).

2. **Capitalism:** an economic system that relies on markets to determine the supply and price of given goods. It assumes that people are rational actors who make decisions based on what benefits them most.

3. **Categorical imperative:** in the philosopher Immanuel Kant's moral theory, categorical imperatives correspond to the idea that certain moral duties are determined by our nature as rational moral beings and as such are always and universally (categorically) valid, ordering what we should do on the basis of a criterion of rationality.

4. **Civil Rights Act:** a 1964 law that formally forbade discrimination on the basis of sex and race in housing, employment, education, and other public settings in the United States. Crucially, it put in place a number of protections to ensure minorities would be able to vote in fair elections.

5. **Civil rights movement:** a struggle beginning in the 1950s in the United States to achieve racial justice and equality. Many of its key moments occurred in the 1960s, including the speeches of Malcolm X and Martin Luther King, Jr., as well as the passage of the Civil Rights Act.

6. **Cold War (1947–89):** a period of tension between the United States and the Soviet Union. While the two countries never engaged in direct military conflict, they engaged in covert and proxy wars and espionage against one another.

7. **Communitarianism:** a current of political theory that emerged as a reaction to the rise of liberal political theory, especially after the publication of Rawls's *A Theory of Justice*. Communitarians are critical of various aspects of liberal individualism and in particular of the idea of an autonomous human being capable of developing a moral conception independently of the society and community to which they naturally belong.

8. **Constitutionalism:** the study of constitutions, particularly written constitutions, but also the belief that each state or society is governed by a certain basic set

of values from which all other law is derived.

9. **Contractarianism:** a key branch of Western political theory. It is based on the idea that human beings agree on the condition of social life by becoming part of a hypothetical contract among themselves, in which they agree on the rules and conditions for living together in a society. Some of the main thinkers in this tradition are Thomas Hobbes (1588–1679), John Locke (1632–1704), Immanuel Kant (1724–1804), and Jean-Jacques Rousseau (1712–78).

10. **Cosmopolitanism:** a branch of liberal political theory particularly characterized by its universalism and commitment to the idea of a universal form of citizenship. The word "cosmopolitan" (which literally means "citizen of the world") dates back to classic Greek philosophy, when Stoic philosophers proposed the idea that humans are in fact citizens of the world.

11. **Democratization:** the process by which states give more power to their citizens in the organization of state institutions and the election of their leaders.

12. **Development:** also called human development, this is a field that promotes well-being in societies lacking economic, educational, and other resources required to be self-sufficient and minimally prosperous.

13. **Difference principle (principle of difference):** the second principle that Rawls lists in his theory of justice. This principle proposes that an unequal distribution of goods in a just society can be tolerated only as far as this distribution is beneficial to the least advantaged persons of that society and that they are attached to offices and positions that are open to all. This principle constitutes the egalitarian component of Rawls's theory of justice and is formulated in various forms across the book.

14. **Enlightenment:** a Western European intellectual current of the mid-1600s to the early 1800s characterized by a movement towards rationality over superstition and for its belief that education and knowledge could improve the human condition.

| Glossary of Terms

15. **Global redistributive tax:** a theoretical tax suggested by Thomas Pogge, which would allow the world to be more just by moving resources to those states and societies that have been previously disadvantaged or impoverished.

16. **Globalization:** the process by which political, cultural, and economic structures are becoming more unified around the world. Due to improvements in technology, travel, international business, and global media, many people argue that globalization is becoming more and more pronounced.

17. **Hiroshima:** with Nagasaki, the site of one of the two atomic bomb attacks in the history of warfare; both are Japanese cities. The use of the atomic bomb was seen as a necessary evil to force Japan to surrender and bring an end to World War II in the Pacific region. Scholars and society continue to fiercely debate the ethics and necessity of this action.

18. **Holocaust:** an event considered to be one of the low points of human history. During World War II, the Nazis and their collaborators killed over 11 million people in a systematized and highly organized fashion. Some six million of these people were killed simply for being Jewish. Other groups targeted for extermination included Roma ("gypsies"), homosexuals, and people suffering from physical and mental disabilities.

19. **Human rights:** generally argued to be universal, these are rights that exist simply by virtue of being human. Various laws and treaties exist to advance and protect these rights, which include things like the right to be a citizen, freedom to participate in government, fair trials, and so on.

20. **Industrial Age:** a period beginning in the mid-1700s and extending into the 1900s, which saw the rapid development of machinery, markets, mass production, and other technologies that radically transformed daily life and society.

21. **Intuitionism:** according to Rawls, "the doctrine that there is an irreducible family of first principles which have to be weighed against one another by asking ourselves which balance, in our considered judgment, is the most

just." In intuitionism there is no priority rule or method that allows conflicts between one principle of justice and another to be balanced; this balancing between principles is to be done by intuition.

22. **Justice as fairness:** the conception according to which the principles that define justice are agreed upon on the basis of a procedure that would be considered fair by anyone, in the sense that they lead to conclusions that would be considered legitimate by any reasonable person, independent of any contingent aspect. To achieve the conditions of fairness, Rawls develops the thought experiment of the original position and its related concepts.

23. **Kilei Ridge:** A battle site in the Philippines where Rawls fought in World War II. It was here that he heard a sermon preached by a pastor who said that God directed the bullets of the Allied forces at the Japanese. This caused Rawls to deeply question, and ultimately reject, his Christian faith.

24. **League of Women Voters:** an organization in the United States founded to encourage women to claim positions of influence in the nation's civic structure. It was founded shortly after women in the United States were permitted to vote.

25. **Liberalism:** one of the most relevant political theories of Western culture. It has its foundations in the Enlightenment of the eighteenth century and is primarily linked to thinkers such as Immanuel Kant and John Locke, among others. Its historical foundation is linked with individual emancipation of free citizens especially in the French Revolution (1789)—a period of great political reform in France in which the monarchy was overthrown and government democratized. Its central concern is with the justification of political institutions that protect the individual freedom of the person against the interference of other persons and in particular political institutions and leaders.

26. **Libertarianism:** a sub-category of liberal political theory which is greatly concerned with the principles of individual freedom and especially negative freedom—the freedom of a person from external interferences. A key element of libertarian thinking is the inalienable right of the individual to

property, which libertarians such as Robert Nozick consider of fundamental importance; for this reason, they criticize forms of distributive justice (the distribution of wealth with the aim of securing social justice).

27. **Nazis (National Socialist Party):** a far-right political party led by Adolf Hitler, which ruled Germany from 1933 to 1945. They believed in a superior Aryan (Germanic) race and were responsible for systematically killing over 11 million people in the Holocaust. They were especially opposed to Jewish people, as well as the disabled, homosexuals, and Roma Gypsy people.

28. **Original position:** The original position is a thought experiment proposed by Rawls to justify the two principles that are established by his theory of justice. The thought experiment begins with the questions: If a rational person had a blank canvas to create a new society, what would they want that society to achieve? How could they best create a society that meets these goals?

29. **Pluralism:** a political system that can accommodate people from a number of different backgrounds, especially in terms of ethnicity or religion. It aims to provide equal rights for all citizens and to ensure that individuals are free to act according to their consciences, all while promoting social harmony between these groups.

30. **Political philosophy:** a subcategory of philosophy specifically concerned with developing theories about the social lives of human beings and the norms and institutions that regulate them. Philosophical speculation about politics is among the oldest. In the Western tradition, political philosophy goes back to the ancient Greek philosophers Plato and Aristotle.

31. **Psychology:** the study of the human mind and how it works to influence human beliefs, behaviors, and decisions.

32. **Reflective equilibrium:** a concept that describes the way in which persons develop their considered convictions of justice by going back and forth from their consolidated principles to reevaluated considerations and then reaching a point of equilibrium.

33. **Social contract:** the idea that society creates a state and gives up some

individual freedoms in exchange for security and the protection of predefined political rights.

34. **Soviet Union:** the Union of Soviet Socialist Republics (USSR), made up of several sub-nations between 1922 and 1991.

35. **State of nature:** an imagined representation of how human society would be in its natural state, without government interference. Hobbes famously argued it would be violent and terrible; thinkers like Rousseau argue people are naturally peaceful.

36. **Teleology:** a view of knowledge that believes in a predefined end or goal to history.

37. **Thought experiments:** tools used by philosophers to create an imaginary situation that allows them to prove a particular point is logical or a certain conclusion would be likely in a given set of circumstances. Examples include Hobbes's "state of nature" and Rawls's "original position."

38. **Toleration:** a political value that argues that society should accept differences that do not cause material harm to other individuals.

39. **Utilitarianism:** a theory according to which utility and happiness should be the main criteria of judgment for moral decisions, and these should be considered in an aggregated measure when thinking of societies, so justifying policies that may maximize collective utility but are detrimental to individual rights and well-being.

40. **Veil of ignorance:** an imaginary condition under which the person operating in the original position makes decisions and reasons about justice, not knowing their social condition, such as social status or class; their natural gifts, such as intelligence, strengths, or abilities; or their individual moral preferences.

41. **Vietnam War:** a Cold War conflict that took place between 1955 and 1975. Considered one of the most controversial events in contemporary US history, it has profoundly influenced the political debate in the United States.

42. **World War II:** a conflict fought in the years 1939–1945 that involved virtually every major country on earth. Fought between the Allies (the United States, Britain, France, the Soviet Union and others), and the Axis (Germany, Italy and Japan, along with their allies), it was seen as a major moral struggle between freedom and tyranny and included seminal events like the Holocaust.

 **PEOPLE MENTIONED IN THE TEXT**

1. **Brian Barry (1936–2009)** was a British philosopher who taught at the London School of Economics and Columbia University. Although friends with Rawls, he critiqued his work in the well-regarded book *The Liberal Critique of Justice* (1972).

2. **Charles Beitz (b. 1949)** is an American political theorist who has written several studies on human rights and issues of global justice. One of his most influential publications is *Political Theory and International Relations*, in which he proposes a cosmopolitan political theory.

3. **Jeremy Bentham (1748–1832)** is the most famous thinker of utilitarianism. His maxim that society should strive to achieve the "greatest good for the greatest number" was highly influential in political and philosophical movements for over 100 years following his death. He was active in a number of social spheres, including prison reform, education, and welfare.

4. **Isaiah Berlin (1909–97)** was a prominent figure of liberal thought in the English-speaking world and elsewhere. He is most commonly known for his distinction between negative and positive freedom, among other contributions to the discipline.

5. **Bill Clinton (b. 1946)** was the 42nd president of the United States. His approach to government and social justice would have made him sympathetic to many of Rawls's aims.

6. **Gerald Cohen (1941–2009)** was an influential Marxist philosopher, the author of several publications that were critical of liberal political theory from a socialist perspective. His work is extensive but some of the most relevant critical observation on Rawls can be found in *Rescuing Justice and Equality* (2008).

7. **Samuel Freeman** is a professor at Pennsylvania University and author of several publications, including one of the most popular commentaries on Rawls's philosophical work, *Rawls* (2007).

8. **Stuart Hampshire (1914–2004)** was an influential philosopher and political thinker known for various publications, such as his study of Spinoza, and his anti-rationalist views on public ethics, expressed in *Thought and Action* and

Justice Is Conflict.

9. **Jonathan Harrison (1924–2014)** was an English philosopher who taught at a number of universities. He is well known for his book *Our Knowledge of Right and Wrong*.

10. **Henry Roy Forbes Harrod (1900–1978)** was an English economist who created a number of novel theories in response to economic liberalism. He also is famous for his biography of the economist John Maynard Keynes.

11. **Herbert Lionel Adolphus Hart (1907–92)** was an influential philosopher of the law based in Oxford and then at the London School of Economics and Political Science, among other major academic centers. He is the author of one of the earliest replies to Rawls's theories.

12. **Thomas Hobbes (1588–1679)** was an English philosopher whose major work, *Leviathan*, famously used the thought experiment of a "state of nature" where people live without a state to argue that such a situation would be the worst possible for society. Instead, he advocates the creation of a social contract in which people living in total freedom willingly give up some of that freedom to a sovereign power in order to gain order and security.

13. **Nien-hê Hsieh** is an associate professor of business administration at Harvard Business School. His work considers questions such as whether profit-seeking corporations can be good for society.

14. **David Hume (1711–76)** was one of the most important philosophers of the Scottish Enlightenment. He argued that people should base their morality on the usefulness, or utility, of their actions in achieving pleasure or gain for themselves and society. In this sense, he is the founder of the utilitarian school of political philosophy.

15. **Lyndon B. Johnson (1908–73)** was the 36th president of the United States. He came to power after the assassination of President Kennedy and continued many of his policies, including the Vietnam War, which he greatly expanded, and the extension of civil rights for racial minorities.

16. **Immanuel Kant (1724–1804)** was one of the founding fathers of Western

modern philosophical thought, known for a number of crucial publications and epitomizing the Enlightenment tradition. He was a forceful proponent of rationality, argued in favor of the need for republican government, and advocated individual political rights.

17. **Oluf Langhelle** is a professor at the University of Stavanger in Norway. He studies sustainable development, corporate social responsibility, political theory, globalization, and a number of other topics that relate to many of Rawls's concerns.

18. **John Locke (1632–1704)** was one of the most influential thinkers of the English-speaking world and of the Enlightenment well known for several intellectual contributions, including the *Two Treatises on Government* (1689).

19. **Alasdair MacIntyre (b. 1929)** is a philosopher especially known for his clear communitarian stance, presented in *After Virtue* and then developed further in subsequent publications.

20. **Norman Malcolm (1911–90)** was an American philosopher. He worked with Ludwig Wittgenstein while at Cambridge University.

21. **Thomas Nagel (b. 1937)** is an influential political philosopher at New York University, known for several of his publications on political theory and philosophy, and especially for his critique of reductionism.

22. **Onora O'Neill (b. 1941)** is an influential Kantian philosopher, now also a member of the House of Lords and a professor at the University of Cambridge.

23. **Robert Nozick (1938–2002)** was an important political theorist primarily associated with the liberal sub-class of libertarianism. He was the author of a debated critique of Rawls's theory, critical of principles of social justice and redistribution above all.

24. **Plato (429–347 B.C.E.)** is one of the most influential and famous philosophers of all time. His book *The Republic* has been a major influence on political thinkers ever since antiquity. Amongst his most important political ideas are that it is possible to imagine an ideal state that can advance a pre-

defined "good life."

25. **Thomas Pogge (b. 1953)** is a professor of political science at Columbia University and one of the youngest students of Rawls. He is known for his theory of global justice, advocating principles of global redistribution.

26. **Jean-Jacques Rousseau (1712–78)** was a leading thinker of the Enlightenment, and among the inspirational sources of the French Revolution. His political-theory work of highest relevance is about the idea of the social contract.

27. **Michael Sandel (b. 1953)** is an American political philosopher at Harvard University. He is best known for his critique of Rawls's theory of justice in *Liberalism and the Limits of Justice* (1998). More recently, he became popular for an innovative course on justice which has been widely publicized in the media and is also available online.

28. **Thomas Scanlon (b. 1940)** is the Alford Professor of Natural Religion, Moral Philosophy, and Civil Polity at Harvard University. He is one of the leading scholars of moral and political philosophy, although his initial academic training was in mathematics. Among his most influential publications are *The Difficulty of Tolerance: Essays in Political Philosophy* (2003) and *What We Owe to Each Other* (1998).

29. **Amartya Sen (b. 1933)** is a philosopher and an economist, a Nobel Prize laureate who has published extensively on a number of topics, often at the crossroads between philosophy and economics. He is known as the founder of the idea of human development and the "capability approach," which have subsequently become influential in the assessment of poverty at the United Nations. One of his most recent works is a comprehensive treatise on justice in which he presents several arguments critical of Rawls's theory.

30. **Judith Shklar (1928–92)** was a political theorist at Harvard University. In her work she wrote about injustice, political evils, and the "liberalism of fear."

31. **Henry Sidgwick (1838–1900)** was an English philosopher in the utilitarian tradition. His work is often seen as the most sophisticated development of

the earlier thought of people like Bentham, who shared his belief that society must strive to provide "the greatest good for the greatest number."

32. **Adam Smith (1723–90)** was a Scottish philosopher and arguably the father of modern economics. His most famous work, *The Wealth of Nations*, speaks about the market as the "invisible hand" which helps to ensure that goods are distributed as efficiently as possible in society. His work is central to many politically liberal concepts about the relationship between the state, business, and citizens.

33. **Charles Taylor (b. 1931)** is one of the most influential contemporary philosophers, known particularly for his work on Hegel. His critique of liberal political theory can be found in *Human Agency and Language: Philosophical Papers 1* (1985).

34. **Paul Weithman** is professor of political philosophy at the University of Notre Dame. He has studied at Harvard under the direction of Rawls and Shklar and is the author of several publications on political theory, particularly on Rawls's political liberalism.

35. **Ludwig Wittgenstein (1889–1951)** was an Austrian philosopher who was especially interested in the role that language plays in human thought, its possibilities, and its limits.

WORKS CITED

1. Barry, Brian. *The Liberal Theory of Justice: A Critical Examination of the Principal Doctrines in "A Theory of Justice" by John Rawls*. Oxford: Clarendon Press, 1973.

2. ———. *Theories of Justice*. Hemel Hempstead: Harvester Wheatsheaf, 1989.

3. Beitz, Charles R. *The Idea of Human Rights*. Oxford: Oxford University Press, 2009.

4. ———. *Political Theory and International Relations*, 2nd ed. Princeton, N. J.: Princeton University Press, 1999.

5. Berkowitz, Peter. "The Ambiguities of Rawls's Influence." *Perspectives on Politics* 4, no. 1 (2006): 121–33.

6. Berlin, Isaiah, and Henry Hardy. *The Crooked Timber of Humanity: Chapters in the History of Ideas*. London: John Murray, 1990.

7. Brown, Chris. "On Amartya Sen and the *Idea of Justice*." *Ethics & International Affairs* 24, no. 3 (2010): 309–18.

8. Buckler, Steve, and David P. Dolowitz. "Theorizing the Third Way: New Labour and Social Justice." *Journal of Political Ideologies* 5, no. 3 (2000): 301–20.

9. Caney, Simon. *Justice beyond Borders: A Global Political Theory*. Oxford: Oxford University Press, 2005.

10. Clark, Barry, and Herbert Gintis. "Rawlsian Justice and Economic Systems." *Philosophy & Public Affairs* (1978): 302–25.

11. Clinton, William J. *Public Papers of Presidents of the United States: William J. Clinton* (1999).

12. Cohen, G. A. *Rescuing Justice and Equality*. Cambridge, MA: Harvard University Press, 2008.

13. Freeman, Samuel Richard. *Rawls*. London: Routledge, 2007.

14. Gregory, Eric. "Before the Original Position: The Neo Orthodox Theology of the Young John Rawls." *Journal of Religious Ethics* 35, no. 2 (2007): 195–6.

15. Hampshire, Stuart. *Spinoza*. Harmondsworth: Pelican; New York: Penguin, 1988.

16. ———. *Thought and Action*. London: Chatto & Windus, 1959.

17. Hart, H. L. A. *The Concept of Law*. Oxford: Clarendon Press, 1961.

18. ———. "Rawls on Liberty and Its Priority." *University of Chicago Law Review*

40, no. 3 (1973): 534–55.

19. Hodgson, Louis-Philippe. "Why the Basic Structure?" *Canadian Journal of Philosophy* 42, no. 3–4 (2012): 303–4.

20. Hsieh, Nien-hê. "The Obligations of Transnational Corporations: Rawlsian Justice and the Duty of Assistance." *Business Ethics Quarterly* 14, no. 4 (2004): 643–61.

21. Kuper, Andrew. "Rawlsian Global Justice: Beyond the Law of Peoples to a Cosmopolitan Law of Persons." *Political Theory* 28, no. 5 (2000): 640–74.

22. Langhelle, Oluf. "Sustainable Development and Social Justice: Expanding the Rawlsian Framework of Global Justice." *Environmental Values* 9, no. 3 (2000): 295–323.

23. Locke, John. *Locke on Toleration*. Edited by Richard Vernon. Cambridge: Cambridge University Press, 2010.

24. ———. *Two Treatises of Government*. Edited by Peter Laslett. Cambridge: Cambridge University Press, 1988.

25. MacIntyre, Alasdair C. *After Virtue: A Study in Moral Theory*, 3rd ed. Notre Dame, IN: University of Notre Dame Press, 2007.

26. ———. *Whose Justice? Which Rationality?* London: Duckworth, 1988.

27. Nagel, Thomas. "The Problem of Global Justice." *Philosophy & Public Affairs* 33, no. 2 (2005): 113–47.

28. Nozick, Robert. "Distributive Justice." *Philosophy & Public Affairs* 3, no. 1 (1973): 45–126.

29. ———. *Anarchy, State, and Utopia*. Oxford: Blackwell, 1974.

30. Pogge, Thomas W. "Eradicating Systemic Poverty: Brief for a Global Resources Dividend." *Journal of Human Development* 2, no. 1 (2001): 59–77.

31. ———. *Realizing Rawls*. Ithaca, N. Y.: Cornell University Press, 1989.

32. ———. *World Poverty and Human Rights: Cosmopolitan Responsibilities and Reforms*, 2nd ed. Cambridge: Polity, 2008.

33. Pogge, Thomas, and Michelle Kosch. *John Rawls: His Life and Theory of Justice*. Oxford: Oxford University Press, 2007.

34. Rawls, John. *Collected Papers*. Edited by Samuel Richard Freeman. Cambridge, MA: Harvard University Press, 1999.

35. ——. "50 Years after Hiroshima." *Dissent* (summer 1995): 323–7.
36. ——. "Justice as Fairness." *Philosophical Review* 67, no. 2 (1958): 164–94.
37. ——. *The Law of Peoples: With "The Idea of Public Reason Revisited"*. Cambridge, MA: Harvard University Press, 1999.
38. ——. *Political Liberalism*. New York: Columbia University Press, 1993.
39. ——. *A Theory of Justice*, rev. ed. Cambridge, MA: Belknap Press of Harvard University Press, 1999.
40. Rousseau, Jean-Jacques. *The Social Contract and Other Later Political Writings*. Edited by Victor Gourevitch. Cambridge: Cambridge University Press, 1997.
41. Sandel, Michael J. *Liberalism and the Limits of Justice*, 2nd ed. Cambridge: Cambridge University Press, 1998.
42. ——. "The Procedural Republic and the Unencumbered Self." *Political Theory* 12, no. 1 (1984): 81–96.
43. Scanlon, Thomas. *The Difficulty of Tolerance: Essays in Political Philosophy*. Cambridge: Cambridge University Press, 2003.

44. ——. *What We Owe to Each Other*. Cambridge, MA: Belknap Press of Harvard University Press, 1998.
45. Sen, Amartya. *Development as Freedom*. Oxford: Oxford University Press, 2001.
46. ——. *The Idea of Justice*. Cambridge, MA: Belknap Press of Harvard University Press, 2009.
47. ——. *Inequality Reexamined*. Oxford: Clarendon Press, 1992.
48. Shklar, Judith. "Giving Injustice Its Due." *Yale Law Journal* 98, no. 6 (1989): 1135–51.
49. Shklar, Judith N., and Stanley Hoffmann. *Political Thought and Political Thinkers*. Chicago: University of Chicago Press, 1998.
50. Taylor, Charles. *Human Agency and Language: Philosophical Papers 1*. Cambridge: Cambridge University Press, 1985.
51. Weithman, Paul J. *Why Political Liberalism? On John Rawls's Political Turn*. New York: Oxford University Press, 2011.

原书作者简介

约翰·罗尔斯，美国哲学家，1921 年出生于一个中上阶层的基督徒家庭。在他小的时候，他的两个兄弟相继去世。后来，在第二次世界大战期间参军，目睹了核弹毁灭广岛后的惨状。罗尔斯放弃了宗教信仰，回归平民生活，相信人生既短暂又不公正。但他同时相信，人类的努力可以使人生变得更加公平。于是，他将职业生涯奉献给了正义研究。2002 年去世，享年 81 岁。

本书作者简介

菲利波·迪奥尼基，获得伦敦政治经济学院博士学位。他目前是该院利弗休姆国际关系青年研究员。著有《真主党、伊斯兰政治和国际社会》（帕尔格雷夫·麦克米兰出版社，2014）。

杰里米·克莱多斯蒂获得圣安德鲁斯大学国际关系博士学位。他目前是于韦斯屈莱大学的博士后研究员。著有《文明音乐会：西方和伊斯兰宪法主义的共同根源》。

世界名著中的批判性思维

《世界思想宝库钥匙丛书》致力于深入浅出地阐释全世界著名思想家的观点，不论是谁、在何处都能了解到，从而推进批判性思维发展。

《世界思想宝库钥匙丛书》与世界顶尖大学的一流学者合作，为一系列学科中最有影响的著作推出新的分析文本，介绍其观点和影响。在这一不断扩展的系列中，每种选入的著作都代表了历经时间考验的思想典范。通过为这些著作提供必要背景、揭示原作者的学术渊源以及说明这些著作所产生的影响，本系列图书希望让读者以新视角看待这些划时代的经典之作。读者应学会思考、运用并挑战这些著作中的观点，而不是简单接受它们。

ABOUT THE AUTHOR OF THE ORIGINAL WORK

Born in 1921, **John Rawls** was an American philosopher from an upper-middle-class Christian family. Two of his brothers died while he was a child. Then, as a soldier during World War II, he saw the horrific effects of the destruction of Hiroshima by nuclear bomb. Rawls returned to civilian life without his faith and with a belief that life was both short and unfair. But he also believed that human endeavor could make life fairer, and dedicated his career to studying justice. He died in 2002 at the age of 81.

ABOUT THE AUTHORS OF THE ANALYSIS

Dr Filippo Dionigi holds a PhD from LSE, where he is currently a Leverhulm Early Career Fellow in International Relations. He is the author of *Hezbollah, Islamist Politics and International Society* (Palgrave MacMillan, 2014).

Dr Jeremy Kleidosty received his PhD in international relations from the University of St Andrews. He is currently a postdoctoral fellow at the University of Jväskylä, and is the author of *The Concert of Civilizations: The Common Roots of Western and Islamic Constitutionalism.*

ABOUT MACAT
GREAT WORKS FOR CRITICAL THINKING

Macat is focused on making the ideas of the world's great thinkers accessible and comprehensible to everybody, everywhere, in ways that promote the development of enhanced critical thinking skills.

It works with leading academics from the world's top universities to produce new analyses that focus on the ideas and the impact of the most influential works ever written across a wide variety of academic disciplines. Each of the works that sit at the heart of its growing library is an enduring example of great thinking. But by setting them in context—and looking at the influences that shaped their authors, as well as the responses they provoked—Macat encourages readers to look at these classics and game-changers with fresh eyes. Readers learn to think, engage and challenge their ideas, rather than simply accepting them.

批判性思维与《正义论》

首要批判性思维技能：理性化思维

次要批判性思维技能：评估

约翰·罗尔斯的《正义论》是第二次世界大战以来发表的最具影响力的法律和政治理论著作之一。它提供了一个令人难忘、构建完善的持久论点，支持给社会正义下新的（社会契约）定义。在阐述这一论点时，罗尔斯旨在构建一个切实可行的系统学说，旨在确保最大化善的过程意识连贯，于是，有了一部突出批判性思维技能的推理著作。罗尔斯重点讨论了现有制度缺点的同时，也解释了他自己的新正义论。

通过阐述他如何得出他的结论，并明确地解释和证明他自己的自由主义的多元价值观，罗尔斯能够提出一个构建完备且完全致力于劝导需要的论点。罗尔斯明确地解释了他的目标。他讨论了其他定义公正社会的方法，并通过解释他对反对观点的反驳来处理反对观点。然后，他仔细而有条理地定义了一些概念和工具——"思想实验"——帮助读者理解他的推理并验证他的思想。罗尔斯的假设是：其有关正义的思想可以普遍应用，即任何时候，任何社会都可以理性地接受。

CRITICAL THINKING AND *A THEORY OF JUSTICE*

- Primary critical thinking skill: REASONING
- Secondary critical thinking skill: EVALUATION

John Rawls's *A Theory of Justice* is one of the most influential works of legal and political theory published since the Second World War. It provides a memorably well-constructed and sustained argument in favour of a new (social contract) version of the meaning of social justice. In setting out this argument, Rawls aims to construct a viable, systematic doctrine designed to ensure that the process of maximizing good is both conscious and coherent—and the result is a work that foregrounds the critical thinking skill of reasoning. Rawls's focus falls equally on discussions of the failings of existing systems and on explanation of his own new theory of justice.

By illustrating how he arrived at his conclusions, and by clearly explaining and justifying his own liberal, pluralist values, Rawls is able to produce a well-structured argument that is fully focused on the need to persuade. Rawls explicitly explains his goals. He discusses other ways of conceptualizing a just society and deals with counter-arguments by explaining his objections to them. Then, carefully and methodically, he defines a number of concepts and tools—"thought experiments"—that help the reader to follow his reasoning and test his ideas. Rawls's hypothesis is that his ideas about justice can be universally applied: they can be accepted as rational in any society at any time.

《世界思想宝库钥匙丛书》简介

《世界思想宝库钥匙丛书》致力于为一系列在各领域产生重大影响的人文社科类经典著作提供独特的学术探讨。每一本读物都不仅仅是原经典著作的内容摘要，而是介绍并深入研究原经典著作的学术渊源、主要观点和历史影响。这一丛书的目的是提供一套学习资料，以促进读者掌握批判性思维，从而更全面、深刻地去理解重要思想。

每一本读物分为3个部分：学术渊源、学术思想和学术影响，每个部分下有4个小节。这些章节旨在从各个方面研究原经典著作及其反响。

由于独特的体例，每一本读物不但易于阅读，而且另有一项优点：所有读物的编排体例相同，读者在进行某个知识层面的调查或研究时可交叉参阅多本该丛书中的相关读物，从而开启跨领域研究的路径。

为了方便阅读，每本读物最后还列出了术语表和人名表（在书中则以星号＊标记），此外还有参考文献。

《世界思想宝库钥匙丛书》与剑桥大学合作，理清了批判性思维的要点，即如何通过6种技能来进行有效思考。其中3种技能让我们能够理解问题，另3种技能让我们有能力解决问题。这6种技能合称为"批判性思维PACIER模式"，它们是：

分析：了解如何建立一个观点；
评估：研究一个观点的优点和缺点；
阐释：对意义所产生的问题加以理解；
创造性思维：提出新的见解，发现新的联系；
解决问题：提出切实有效的解决办法；
理性化思维：创建有说服力的观点。

THE MACAT LIBRARY

The Macat Library is a series of unique academic explorations of seminal works in the humanities and social sciences — books and papers that have had a significant and widely recognised impact on their disciplines. It has been created to serve as much more than just a summary of what lies between the covers of a great book. It illuminates and explores the influences on, ideas of, and impact of that book. Our goal is to offer a learning resource that encourages critical thinking and fosters a better, deeper understanding of important ideas.

Each publication is divided into three Sections: Influences, Ideas, and Impact. Each Section has four Modules. These explore every important facet of the work, and the responses to it.

This Section-Module structure makes a Macat Library book easy to use, but it has another important feature. Because each Macat book is written to the same format, it is possible (and encouraged!) to cross-reference multiple Macat books along the same lines of inquiry or research. This allows the reader to open up interesting interdisciplinary pathways.

To further aid your reading, lists of glossary terms and people mentioned are included at the end of this book (these are indicated by an asterisk [*] throughout) — as well as a list of works cited.

Macat has worked with the University of Cambridge to identify the elements of critical thinking and understand the ways in which six different skills combine to enable effective thinking.

Three allow us to fully understand a problem; three more give us the tools to solve it. Together, these six skills make up the PACIER model of critical thinking. They are:

ANALYSIS — understanding how an argument is built
EVALUATION — exploring the strengths and weaknesses of an argument
INTERPRETATION — understanding issues of meaning
CREATIVE THINKING — coming up with new ideas and fresh connections
PROBLEM-SOLVING — producing strong solutions
REASONING — creating strong arguments

"《世界思想宝库钥匙丛书》提供了独一无二的跨学科学习和研究工具。它介绍那些革新了各自学科研究的经典著作,还邀请全世界一流专家和教育机构进行严谨的分析,为每位读者打开世界顶级教育的大门。"

——安德烈亚斯·施莱歇尔,
经济合作与发展组织教育与技能司司长

"《世界思想宝库钥匙丛书》直面大学教育的巨大挑战……他们组建了一支精干而活跃的学者队伍,来推出在研究广度上颇具新意的教学材料。"

——布罗尔斯教授、勋爵,剑桥大学前校长

"《世界思想宝库钥匙丛书》的愿景令人赞叹。它通过分析和阐释那些曾深刻影响人类思想以及社会、经济发展的经典文本,提供了新的学习方法。它推动批判性思维,这对于任何社会和经济体来说都是至关重要的。这就是未来的学习方法。"

——查尔斯·克拉克阁下,英国前教育大臣

"对于那些影响了各自领域的著作,《世界思想宝库钥匙丛书》能让人们立即了解到围绕那些著作展开的评论性言论,这让该系列图书成为在这些领域从事研究的师生们不可或缺的资源。"

——威廉·特朗佐教授,加利福尼亚大学圣地亚哥分校

"Macat offers an amazing first-of-its-kind tool for interdisciplinary learning and research. Its focus on works that transformed their disciplines and its rigorous approach, drawing on the world's leading experts and educational institutions, opens up a world-class education to anyone."

—— Andreas Schleicher, Director for Education and Skills, Organisation for Economic Co-operation and Development

"Macat is taking on some of the major challenges in university education... They have drawn together a strong team of active academics who are producing teaching materials that are novel in the breadth of their approach."

—— Prof Lord Broers, former Vice-Chancellor of the University of Cambridge

"The Macat vision is exceptionally exciting. It focuses upon new modes of learning which analyse and explain seminal texts which have profoundly influenced world thinking and so social and economic development. It promotes the kind of critical thinking which is essential for any society and economy. This is the learning of the future."

—— Rt Hon Charles Clarke, former UK Secretary of State for Education

"The Macat analyses provide immediate access to the critical conversation surrounding the books that have shaped their respective discipline, which will make them an invaluable resource to all of those, students and teachers, working in the field."

—— Prof William Tronzo, University of California at San Diego

The Macat Library
世界思想宝库钥匙丛书

TITLE	中文书名	类别
An Analysis of Arjun Appadurai's *Modernity at Large: Cultural Dimensions of Globalisation*	解析阿尔君·阿帕杜莱《消失的现代性：全球化的文化维度》	人类学
An Analysis of Claude Lévi-Strauss's *Structural Anthropology*	解析克劳德·列维-斯特劳斯《结构人类学》	人类学
An Analysis of Marcel Mauss's *The Gift*	解析马塞尔·莫斯《礼物》	人类学
An Analysis of Jared M. Diamond's *Guns, Germs, and Steel: The Fate of Human Societies*	解析贾雷德·戴蒙德《枪炮、病菌与钢铁：人类社会的命运》	人类学
An Analysis of Clifford Geertz's *The Interpretation of Cultures*	解析克利福德·格尔茨《文化的解释》	人类学
An Analysis of Philippe Ariès's *Centuries of Childhood: A Social History of Family Life*	解析菲力浦·阿利埃斯《儿童的世纪：旧制度下的儿童和家庭生活》	人类学
An Analysis of W. Chan Kim & Renée Mauborgne's *Blue Ocean Strategy*	解析金伟灿/勒妮·莫博涅《蓝海战略》	商业
An Analysis of John P. Kotter's *Leading Change*	解析约翰·P.科特《领导变革》	商业
An Analysis of Michael E. Porter's *Competitive Strategy: Techniques for Analyzing Industries and Competitors*	解析迈克尔·E.波特《竞争战略：分析产业和竞争对手的技术》	商业
An Analysis of Jean Lave & Etienne Wenger's *Situated Learning: Legitimate Peripheral Participation*	解析琼·莱夫/艾蒂纳·温格《情境学习：合法的边缘性参与》	商业
An Analysis of Douglas McGregor's *The Human Side of Enterprise*	解析道格拉斯·麦格雷戈《企业的人性面》	商业
An Analysis of Milton Friedman's *Capitalism and Freedom*	解析米尔顿·弗里德曼《资本主义与自由》	商业
An Analysis of Ludwig von Mises's *The Theory of Money and Credit*	解析路德维希·冯·米塞斯《货币和信用理论》	经济学
An Analysis of Adam Smith's *The Wealth of Nations*	解析亚当·斯密《国富论》	经济学
An Analysis of Thomas Piketty's *Capital in the Twenty-First Century*	解析托马斯·皮凯蒂《21世纪资本论》	经济学
An Analysis of Nassim Nicholas Taleb's *The Black Swan: The Impact of the Highly Improbable*	解析纳西姆·尼古拉斯·塔勒布《黑天鹅：如何应对不可预知的未来》	经济学
An Analysis of Ha-Joon Chang's *Kicking Away the Ladder*	解析张夏准《富国陷阱：发达国家为何踢开梯子》	经济学
An Analysis of Thomas Robert Malthus's *An Essay on the Principle of Population*	解析托马斯·马尔萨斯《人口论》	经济学

An Analysis of John Maynard Keynes's *The General Theory of Employment, Interest and Money*	解析约翰·梅纳德·凯恩斯《就业、利息和货币通论》	经济学
An Analysis of Milton Friedman's *The Role of Monetary Policy*	解析米尔顿·弗里德曼《货币政策的作用》	经济学
An Analysis of Burton G. Malkiel's *A Random Walk Down Wall Street*	解析伯顿·G. 马尔基尔《漫步华尔街》	经济学
An Analysis of Friedrich A. Hayek's *The Road to Serfdom*	解析弗里德里希·A. 哈耶克《通往奴役之路》	经济学
An Analysis of Charles P. Kindleberger's *Manias, Panics, and Crashes: A History of Financial Crises*	解析查尔斯·P. 金德尔伯格《疯狂、惊恐和崩溃：金融危机史》	经济学
An Analysis of Amartya Sen's *Development as Freedom*	解析阿马蒂亚·森《以自由看待发展》	经济学
An Analysis of Rachel Carson's *Silent Spring*	解析蕾切尔·卡森《寂静的春天》	地理学
An Analysis of Charles Darwin's *On the Origin of Species: by Means of Natural Selection, or The Preservation of Favoured Races in the Struggle for Life*	解析查尔斯·达尔文《物种起源》	地理学
An Analysis of World Commission on Environment and Development's *The Brundtland Report, Our Common Future*	解析世界环境与发展委员会《布伦特兰报告：我们共同的未来》	地理学
An Analysis of James E. Lovelock's *Gaia: A New Look at Life on Earth*	解析詹姆斯·E. 拉伍洛克《盖娅：地球生命的新视野》	地理学
An Analysis of Paul Kennedy's *The Rise and Fall of the Great Powers: Economic Change and Military Conflict from 1500—2000*	解析保罗·肯尼迪《大国的兴衰：1500—2000年的经济变革与军事冲突》	历史
An Analysis of Janet L. Abu-Lughod's *Before European Hegemony: The World System A. D. 1250—1350*	解析珍妮特·L. 阿布-卢格霍德《欧洲霸权之前：1250—1350年的世界体系》	历史
An Analysis of Alfred W. Crosby's *The Columbian Exchange: Biological and Cultural Consequences of 1492*	解析艾尔弗雷德·W. 克罗斯比《哥伦布大交换：1492年以后的生物影响和文化冲击》	历史
An Analysis of Tony Judt's *Postwar: A History of Europe since 1945*	解析托尼·朱特《战后欧洲史》	历史
An Analysis of Richard J. Evans's *In Defence of History*	解析理查德·J. 艾文斯《捍卫历史》	历史
An Analysis of Eric Hobsbawm's *The Age of Revolution: Europe 1789–1848*	解析艾瑞克·霍布斯鲍姆《革命的年代：欧洲1789—1848年》	历史

An Analysis of Roland Barthes's *Mythologies*	解析罗兰·巴特《神话学》	文学与批判理论
An Analysis of Simon de Beauvoir's *The Second Sex*	解析西蒙娜·德·波伏娃《第二性》	文学与批判理论
An Analysis of Edward W. Said's *Orientalism*	解析爱德华·W. 萨义德《东方主义》	文学与批判理论
An Analysis of Virginia Woolf's *A Room of One's Own*	解析弗吉尼亚·伍尔芙《一间自己的房间》	文学与批判理论
An Analysis of Judith Butler's *Gender Trouble*	解析朱迪斯·巴特勒《性别麻烦》	文学与批判理论
An Analysis of Ferdinand de Saussure's *Course in General Linguistics*	解析费尔迪南·德·索绪尔《普通语言学教程》	文学与批判理论
An Analysis of Susan Sontag's *On Photography*	解析苏珊·桑塔格《论摄影》	文学与批判理论
An Analysis of Walter Benjamin's *The Work of Art in the Age of Mechanical Reproduction*	解析瓦尔特·本雅明《机械复制时代的艺术作品》	文学与批判理论
An Analysis of W.E.B. Du Bois's *The Souls of Black Folk*	解析 W.E.B. 杜波依斯《黑人的灵魂》	文学与批判理论
An Analysis of Plato's *The Republic*	解析柏拉图《理想国》	哲学
An Analysis of Plato's *Symposium*	解析柏拉图《会饮篇》	哲学
An Analysis of Aristotle's *Metaphysics*	解析亚里士多德《形而上学》	哲学
An Analysis of Aristotle's *Nicomachean Ethics*	解析亚里士多德《尼各马可伦理学》	哲学
An Analysis of Immanuel Kant's *Critique of Pure Reason*	解析伊曼努尔·康德《纯粹理性批判》	哲学
An Analysis of Ludwig Wittgenstein's *Philosophical Investigations*	解析路德维希·维特根斯坦《哲学研究》	哲学
An Analysis of G.W.F. Hegel's *Phenomenology of Spirit*	解析 G.W.F. 黑格尔《精神现象学》	哲学
An Analysis of Baruch Spinoza's *Ethics*	解析巴鲁赫·斯宾诺莎《伦理学》	哲学
An Analysis of Hannah Arendt's *The Human Condition*	解析汉娜·阿伦特《人的境况》	哲学
An Analysis of G.E.M. Anscombe's *Modern Moral Philosophy*	解析 G.E.M. 安斯康姆《现代道德哲学》	哲学
An Analysis of David Hume's *An Enquiry Concerning Human Understanding*	解析大卫·休谟《人类理解研究》	哲学

An Analysis of Søren Kierkegaard's *Fear and Trembling*	解析索伦·克尔凯郭尔《恐惧与战栗》	哲学
An Analysis of René Descartes's *Meditations on First Philosophy*	解析勒内·笛卡尔《第一哲学沉思录》	哲学
An Analysis of Friedrich Nietzsche's *On the Genealogy of Morality*	解析弗里德里希·尼采《论道德的谱系》	哲学
An Analysis of Gilbert Ryle's *The Concept of Mind*	解析吉尔伯特·赖尔《心的概念》	哲学
An Analysis of Thomas Kuhn's *The Structure of Scientific Revolutions*	解析托马斯·库恩《科学革命的结构》	哲学
An Analysis of John Stuart Mill's *Utilitarianism*	解析约翰·斯图亚特·穆勒《功利主义》	哲学
An Analysis of Aristotle's *Politics*	解析亚里士多德《政治学》	政治学
An Analysis of Niccolò Machiavelli's *The Prince*	解析尼科洛·马基雅维利《君主论》	政治学
An Analysis of Karl Marx's *Capital*	解析卡尔·马克思《资本论》	政治学
An Analysis of Benedict Anderson's *Imagined Communities*	解析本尼迪克特·安德森《想象的共同体》	政治学
An Analysis of Samuel P. Huntington's *The Clash of Civilizations and the Remaking of World Order*	解析塞缪尔·P.亨廷顿《文明的冲突与世界秩序重建》	政治学
An Analysis of Alexis de Tocqueville's *Democracy in America*	解析阿列克西·德·托克维尔《论美国的民主》	政治学
An Analysis of John A. Hobson's *Imperialism: A Study*	解析约翰·A.霍布森《帝国主义》	政治学
An Analysis of Thomas Paine's *Common Sense*	解析托马斯·潘恩《常识》	政治学
An Analysis of John Rawls's *A Theory of Justice*	解析约翰·罗尔斯《正义论》	政治学
An Analysis of Francis Fukuyama's *The End of History and the Last Man*	解析弗朗西斯·福山《历史的终结与最后的人》	政治学
An Analysis of John Locke's *Two Treatises of Government*	解析约翰·洛克《政府论》	政治学
An Analysis of Sun Tzu's *The Art of War*	解析孙武《孙子兵法》	政治学
An Analysis of Henry Kissinger's *World Order: Reflections on the Character of Nations and the Course of History*	解析亨利·基辛格《世界秩序》	政治学
An Analysis of Jean-Jacques Rousseau's *The Social Contract*	解析让-雅克·卢梭《社会契约论》	政治学

An Analysis of Odd Arne Westad's *The Global Cold War: Third World Interventions and the Making of Our Times*	解析文安立《全球冷战：美苏对第三世界的干涉与当代世界的形成》	政治学
An Analysis of Sigmund Freud's *The Interpretation of Dreams*	解析西格蒙德·弗洛伊德《梦的解析》	心理学
An Analysis of William James' *The Principles of Psychology*	解析威廉·詹姆斯《心理学原理》	心理学
An Analysis of Philip Zimbardo's *The Lucifer Effect*	解析菲利普·津巴多《路西法效应》	心理学
An Analysis of Leon Festinger's *A Theory of Cognitive Dissonance*	解析利昂·费斯汀格《认知失调论》	心理学
An Analysis of Richard H. Thaler & Cass R. Sunstein's *Nudge: Improving Decisions about Health, Wealth, and Happiness*	解析理查德·H. 泰勒/卡斯·R. 桑斯坦《助推：如何做出有关健康、财富和幸福的更优决策》	心理学
An Analysis of Gordon Allport's *The Nature of Prejudice*	解析高尔登·奥尔波特《偏见的本质》	心理学
An Analysis of Steven Pinker's *The Better Angels of Our Nature: Why Violence Has Declined*	解析斯蒂芬·平克《人性中的善良天使：暴力为什么会减少》	心理学
An Analysis of Stanley Milgram's *Obedience to Authority*	解析斯坦利·米尔格拉姆《对权威的服从》	心理学
An Analysis of Betty Friedan's *The Feminine Mystique*	解析贝蒂·弗里丹《女性的奥秘》	心理学
An Analysis of David Riesman's *The Lonely Crowd: A Study of the Changing American Character*	解析大卫·理斯曼《孤独的人群：美国人社会性格演变之研究》	社会学
An Analysis of Franz Boas's *Race, Language and Culture*	解析弗朗兹·博厄斯《种族、语言与文化》	社会学
An Analysis of Pierre Bourdieu's *Outline of a Theory of Practice*	解析皮埃尔·布尔迪厄《实践理论大纲》	社会学
An Analysis of Max Weber's *The Protestant Ethic and the Spirit of Capitalism*	解析马克斯·韦伯《新教伦理与资本主义精神》	社会学
An Analysis of Jane Jacobs's *The Death and Life of Great American Cities*	解析简·雅各布斯《美国大城市的死与生》	社会学
An Analysis of C. Wright Mills's *The Sociological Imagination*	解析C. 赖特·米尔斯《社会学的想象力》	社会学
An Analysis of Robert E. Lucas Jr.'s *Why Doesn't Capital Flow from Rich to Poor Countries?*	解析小罗伯特·E. 卢卡斯《为何资本不从富国流向穷国？》	社会学

An Analysis of Émile Durkheim's *On Suicide*	解析埃米尔·迪尔凯姆《自杀论》	社会学
An Analysis of Eric Hoffer's *The True Believer: Thoughts on the Nature of Mass Movements*	解析埃里克·霍弗《狂热分子：群众运动圣经》	社会学
An Analysis of Jared M. Diamond's *Collapse: How Societies Choose to Fail or Survive*	解析贾雷德·M.戴蒙德《大崩溃：社会如何选择兴亡》	社会学
An Analysis of Michel Foucault's *The History of Sexuality Vol. 1: The Will to Knowledge*	解析米歇尔·福柯《性史（第一卷）：求知意志》	社会学
An Analysis of Michel Foucault's *Discipline and Punish*	解析米歇尔·福柯《规训与惩罚》	社会学
An Analysis of Richard Dawkins's *The Selfish Gene*	解析理查德·道金斯《自私的基因》	社会学
An Analysis of Antonio Gramsci's *Prison Notebooks*	解析安东尼奥·葛兰西《狱中札记》	社会学
An Analysis of Augustine's *Confessions*	解析奥古斯丁《忏悔录》	神学
An Analysis of C.S. Lewis's *The Abolition of Man*	解析C.S.路易斯《人之废》	神学

图书在版编目（CIP）数据

解析约翰·罗尔斯《正义论》：汉、英／菲利波·迪奥尼基（Filippo Dionigi），杰里米·克莱多斯蒂（Jeremy Kleidosty）著；高伟，高英淇译．
—上海：上海外语教育出版社，2019
（世界思想宝库钥匙丛书）
ISBN 978-7-5446-5951-2

Ⅰ.①解… Ⅱ.①菲… ②杰… ③高… ④高… Ⅲ.①罗尔斯（Rawls, John Bordley 1921-2002）—正义—理论研究—汉、英 Ⅳ.①B712.59

中国版本图书馆CIP数据核字（2019）第152270号

This Chinese-English bilingual edition of *An Analysis of John Rawls's A Theory of Justice* is published by arrangement with MACAT International Limited.
Licensed for sale throughout the world.

本书汉英双语版由Macat国际有限公司授权上海外语教育出版社有限公司出版。
供在全世界范围内发行、销售。

图字：09-2018-549

出版发行：**上海外语教育出版社**
（上海外国语大学内） 邮编：200083
电　　话：021-65425300（总机）
电子邮箱：bookinfo@sflep.com.cn
网　　址：http://www.sflep.com
责任编辑：严　凯

印　　刷：上海叶大印务发展有限公司
开　　本：890×1240　1/32　印张 5.625　字数 115千字
版　　次：2019年9月第1版　2019年9月第1次印刷
印　　数：2 100册

书　　号：ISBN 978-7-5446-5951-2
定　　价：30.00元

本版图书如有印装质量问题，可向本社调换
质量服务热线：4008-213-263　电子邮箱：editorial@sflep.com